BIRMINGHAM BUSES AFTER WITHDRAWAL

DAVID HARVEY

AMBERLEY

View over Bird's scrapyard, Stratford

The view over W. T. Bird's scrapyard in Stratford on 9 August 1953 reveals that the remains of all the last tramcars used on the Erdington group of routes. Stacked with the lower saloons on top of the upper decks, Bird had obtained the contract to dispose of all the remaining 108 tram cars that operated from Miller Street and Witton depots on the last three BCT tram routes. This was the day after tram PW8, the cut-down works car, had arrived on a low loader from Kyotts Lake Road Works. It had been used as the works shunter and was the last tram in Birmingham to move under its own power on the previous day. The tram had been built for the City of Birmingham Tramways Company in 1901 as their 158 and had been built by ER & TCW with a 26/22 seating capacity for use on the CBT's Bristol Road service. After CBT was taken over in 1911 the tram became BCT 505 and was soon converted to a single-deck works car. In the distance on the right are two all-over blue-painted Daimler COG5s. The rear of the bus facing the tram is bus 1021 (CVP 121), delivered on 1 July 1937; it has a MCCW body and had arrived at Bird's early in 1953 and would be broken up by 1957. On the extreme right is the engineless 833 (BOP 833), which had a BRCW body and dated from October 1936. (A. N. H. Glover)

First published 2018

Amberley Publishing
The Hill, Stroud
Gloucestershire, GL5 4EP

www.amberley-books.com

Copyright © David Harvey 2018

The right of David Harvey to be identified as the Author
of this work has been asserted in accordance with the
Copyrights, Designs and Patents Act 1988.

All rights reserved. No part of this book may be reprinted
or reproduced or utilised in any form or by any electronic,
mechanical or other means, now known or hereafter invented,
including photocopying and recording, or in any information
storage or retrieval system, without the permission in writing
from the Publishers.

British Library Cataloguing in Publication Data.
A catalogue record for this book is available from the British Library.

ISBN 978 1 4456 7058 4 (print)
ISBN 978 1 4456 7059 1 (ebook)

Typeset in 10pt on 13pt Sabon.
Typesetting and Origination by Amberley Publishing.
Printed in the UK.

Contents

	Acknowledgements	4
	Introduction	4
	Brief History	5
1	Early Pre-War Withdrawals	8
2	Wartime Disposals of 1930s Stock	14
3	Early Withdrawals of Pre-War Buses	23
4	Later Withdrawals of Pre-War Buses	30
5	Wartime Buses	51
6	Trolleybuses Disposals	59
7	Post-War Buses, 1947–1948	69
8	Post-War Buses, 1949–1950	82
9	Post-War Buses, 1950–1960	97
10	Rear-Engined Buses	115
	Endnote	128
	Bibliography	128

Acknowledgements

The author is grateful to the many photographers acknowledged in the text who have contributed to this volume. I sincerely thank all of those who are still alive for allowing me to use pictures, many of which were taken more than sixty years ago. Thanks are especially due to Alan Broughall, the late Les Mason, the late Les Perkins, P. Tizard and the late Alf Yeates, who all allowed me to print their photographs many years ago and generously gave permission for me to use their material. Where the photographer is not known, the photographs are credited to my own collection. Special thanks are due to my wife, Diana, for her usual advice and splendid proofreading.

The book would not have been possible without the continued encouragement given by Connor Stait and Louis Archard at Amberley Publishing.

Introduction

At what at first seems a depressing title, the withdrawal, storage, disposal and ultimate scrapping of a bus is at once poignant and exhilarating, while having a certain finality about it. A bus that one had seen for years that was about to be taken out of service was like saying goodbye to an old friend. In some cases the demise of a bus might seem premature, but expiring CoFs, mechanical failure or hidden structural faults might have played a part. Suddenly new buses replaced those vehicles with which one had grown up and the old faithful were suddenly missing. So where had they gone?

In many cases a bus was taken out of service as it was just time expired and needed replacing, but in many cases with Birmingham's fleet buses that looked immaculate were driven back into the garage after a day's work, driven into a corner switched-off, de-licensed and withdrawn. Within a few months it was in a dealers yard waiting to be sold on or to have an appointment with the breaker's torch.

This is an attempt to look at all these scenarios while at the same time telling the story of each photographed bus and the reasons that caused its withdrawal.

David Harvey, 2018

Brief History

The disposal of buses is frequently a somewhat clandestine operation. One day your favourite bus is working on the route that it has been associated with for many years and the next day it has disappeared. For a time it languished in the recesses of its former garage gathering dust, and if it hasn't been stripped for spare parts it is dumped in a disposal yard before eventually being collected by either a dealer in second-hand buses or the scrap man.

In Birmingham there were distinct blocks of time when this occurred. Firstly, there was the period in the mid-1930s when the outside staircase buses were replaced, with the preferred dealers being Cunliffe's of Great Bridge and Handsworth. The second period was in the years immediately after the Second World War, when worn-out and abused early 1930s stock needed to be disposed of due, in the main, to a lack of maintenance and bodywork wearing out. In this period, after using Devey of Shenstone in the first two years after the end of the war, Woodfield & Turner of Burnley, who traded under the name of Used Units, were briefly purchasers of withdrawn Birmingham buses. It was said of this company that if a bus was sold to them it never ran again. The main post-war beneficiary of purchasing withdrawn Birmingham buses was W. T. Bird of Stratford-upon-Avon, who not only disposed of all the Coventry Road trolleybus fleet, but from 1949 broke up most of the surviving post-war tramcars. Their long attachment to Birmingham buses lasted from 1948 until the early 1970s but they were most active between 1950 and 1955, and from 1960 until 1968. Unusually, they also acted as sellers into the second-hand bus market as well as scrap dealers.

At the end of the Second World War, the 1943 programme was reintroduced in a slightly modified form and the decision to finally scrap the tram system and take out the still profitable Coventry Road trolleybus fleet was made. This meant that new buses had to be purchased to replace around 441 tramcars and the entire fleet of seventy-four trolleybuses. Additionally, the Transport Department had decided to replace almost all of its pre-war bus fleet and all of the 161 wartime vehicles over a seven-year period. In all, 1,748 new buses came as replacements.

These decisions presaged the beginning of the fourth period of mass bus disposal by Birmingham Corporation Tramways (BCT). A site had to found to store the large numbers of withdrawn buses, as previously used locations, such as alongside bus garages and the quite small area between Western Road and a loop on the Birmingham Canal just of Dudley Road, was obviously inadequate. A huge new site was owned by the City Salvage Department in Holford Drive, Perry Barr, which was made available to the Transport Department for storage prior to disposal of literally hundreds of buses.

Many of the buses were either sold directly to other operators or to dealers, who, after selecting the best ones, sold them on for further use.

Holford Drive was brought into use in 1947 and was used until the early part of 1955, when the last of the pre-war buses (except for a reserve fleet of forty-two of the best Daimler COG5s) were put into store for future contingencies, and thirty-six similar buses were used as snowploughs from 1953 and 1954, until they were all withdrawn en mass on 31 July 1963. Additionally, there were six Guy Arab IIs that were converted to dual-control driver-trainers, with their original wartime bodies having been replaced by bodies taken off previously converted petrol-engined AEC Regent chassis.

Meanwhile, the two closures of the trolleybus system, with the Nechells route going on 30 September 1940 and the Coventry Road routes on 30 June 1951, resulted in two different disposal scenarios. All of the 1932 stock used on the Nechells route were put into storage at the former Sampson Road tram paint shop until 1945 and were sold to Midland Motors, which was located only about a mile from their storage site. At least three of these trolleybuses were sold to be scrapped in Oldbury.

The Coventry Road trolleybus disposals were much more straightforward, with all seventy-four surviving vehicles being sold to Bird's. Bird's undertook to tow the sixty-one trolleybuses behind Second World War former War Department lorries to Stratford-upon-Avon between Saturday 30 June, in the middle of the normal services along Coventry Road, and Sunday 1 July 1951. Some trolleybuses even ran back to Coventry Road depot at the end of their duty and, while the motors were still warm, had their destination blinds removed and were immediately hitched up behind one of Bird's lorries and driven straight off to Stratford. Fourteen of the trolleybuses initially went to Cunliffe's in Handsworth Wood, but within six months these too had arrived in Stratford for scrapping.

The Achilles heel of the plan to replace the bus fleet was that the introduction of a huge new bus fleet between 1947 and 1954 meant that many of the earlier buses became surplus to requirements as the travelling public became more affluent in the late 1950s and bought cars or stayed at home in the evenings to watch the new television stations – a fact that was dramatically increase by the arrival of commercial television. As a result, between 1961 and 1969, when West Midlands PTE took over, many quite serviceable buses were withdrawn.

From this time until the final withdrawals of BCT buses by 1983 under the ownership of WMPTE, there was an increasing use of the plethora of Barnsley and South Yorkshire breakers yards, where very few of the former municipal buses ever escaped. All the exposed radiator buses were eliminated from the fleet during this period, including the early Daimler CVA6s and CVGs, along with most of the Daimler CVD6s. During the same period all the Leyland Titan PD2/1s and Crossley DD42/6s – which, with their manual gearboxes, numbered some 471 vehicles – were also withdrawn. These fifty-four-seat buses were replaced on a nine-for-ten basis with Daimler Fleetline CRG6LXs, of which 559 were purchased in the period from 1962 until 1969, when the same model became the standard double-deck bus for West Midlands PTE.

The second-hand market was effectively closed by the Transport Department after

1963, when a change of policy meant that no bus could be sold on for further use. As Holford Drive had been sold in about 1956, buses were once again parked up alongside garages, with the plot of land adjacent to Washwood Heath Garage being one of the most used pieces of land, as well as Adderley Street yard.

After West Midlands PTE took over the four West Midlands municipal operators on 1 October 1969, it was soon apparent that the long-standing traditions of excellent maintenance and overhauling by Birmingham City Transport enabled many of the nearly 600 Daimler CVG6 and Guy Arab III and IV Specials to continue working until the end of open rear platform buses worked on the Outer Circle 11 route on 31 October 1977. Throughout the 1970s, the buses were sold to numerous Yorkshire scrap dealers in the Barnsley, Carlton and Rotherham area and were stored before disposal mainly at Adderley Street yard, although Lea Hall Garage yard was also used.

I

Early Pre-War Withdrawals

26 (O 9926)
Above: Birmingham Corporation Tramways (BCT) Department took over a total of thirty Tilling-Stevens double-deckers on 5 October 1914 from the Birmingham & Midland Motor Omnibus (BMMO) Company (later Midland Red) as part of their new operating agreement. This agreement allowed the company free access into Birmingham, but without picking up rights within the boundary and the Corporation not encroaching on BMMO territory beyond the city limits. BMMO's operating policy concentrated on single-deckers between towns and therefore had little need for these double-deckers. A total of seventeen Tilling O18/16RO-bodied 40 hp petrol-electric Tilling-Stevens TTA2s were taken over and one of these was 26 (O 9926), which was originally built in March 1913. It was withdrawn on 2 December 1924 and while its chassis was retained, the body was sold privately to a purchaser in Colwick, Nottinghamshire, in 1925. There it remained until the body was salvaged in 1974 before going to Birmingham & Midland Motor Omnibus Trust (BaMMOT) in Wythall for undercover storage and drying out. It would get a slightly later Tilling-Stevens TS3, on which it was mounted in December 2011. It is in the process of being mounted on the acquired chassis on 30 May 1994 and amazingly remnants of the livery, legal lettering and lining out had survived. (D. R. Harvey)

116 (OM 215)
Opposite above: Languishing in a farmer's yard in Herefordshire are the remains of 116 (OM 215), an AEC 504 with a Short H26/26RO body that was first in service on 27 November 1924. Withdrawn on 30 November 1934, it was sold to a dealer named Fitzhugh of West Bromwich, who sold it on as a caravan, and it resided in the Severn Valley until its remains were discovered. This is the lower saloon, whose wooden body frames and ceiling can be identified, and the rear platform. (D. R. Harvey)

Early Pre-War Withdrawals

164 (ON 1315)

Below: Although looking in good condition, 164 (ON 1315) is actually withdrawn and has the city coat of arms on the lower side panel painted out. 164 was a Short Brothers H26/26RO-bodied AEC 504, which had entered service on 4 December 1925. They all had outside staircases and open cabs, which the 'old sweats' preferred, as the later buses with enclosed cabs used to leak and the windscreens misted up. However, with the open cab a heavy tarpaulin could be pulled up from the front cowling and could be attached to the driver's greatcoat, which kept him reasonably dry and his hands warm. 164 is at Cunliffe's scrapyard at Great Bridge in June 1935 and was quickly broken up. (M. Rooum)

168 (ON 1319)
Above: Thomas Cunliffe had a number of scrapyards in the Handsworth Wood area. On 21 April 1943 the former bus 168 (ON 1319), a late 1925-built AEC 504 sold to Cunliffe's in May 1935, stands in their Wellington Road yard. It's original Short H26/26RO bodywork was scrapped on arrival but the chassis was converted to a flatbed lorry and was used by Cunliffe's as their lorry, using the trade plates 230 OP. On the left are tantalising remnants of other broken-up buses bought from Birmingham. (L. W. Perkins)

181 (OP 210)
Opposite above: Eight AEC 504 and ADC 507s are lined up in Cunliffe's yard in the summer of 1935. At least four have open driver's cabs with tarpaulin sheets to protect the drivers. On the left is the open-cabbed 168 (ON 1319), an AEC 504 with a Short H26/26RO body that had entered service on 11 September 1926 and was not withdrawn until 31 May 1935. Next to it is 252 (OX 1518), a slightly later enclosed cab, Short-bodied ADC 507 dating from October 1927. Both buses were taken out of service on 31 May 1935 and sold to Cunliffe on 12 June 1935 for scrapping. The AEC/ADC buses of this vintage were instrumental in the rapid expansion of the 'main road' bus routes in the city and contributed to the 1930s concept of initially not expanding the extensive tram system and later to closing it altogether. (M. Rooum)

213 (OP 3653)
Opposite below: The burnt-out body of Buckingham-bodied AEC 507 213 (OP 3653) looks a sorry sight. It had been destroyed in March 1932 and the remnants of the body frame show that it was of a composite design with the roof sticks, waistrail and supporting angle irons at least being made of steel. The chassis of 213 was retrieved and was converted to a tower wagon using the 1920 tower originally fitted to a 1912 Tilling-Stevens TTA1 chassis. 213 continued to be used as an overhead tower wagon as Service Vehicle 3 until 1948. (B. C. T.)

Early Pre-War Withdrawals

Birmingham Buses after Withdrawal

97 (UK 8047)
Above: Withdrawn in January 1934, the Hall Lewis H24/24R body of BCT demonstrator 97 (UK 8047), was taken off the Guy Invincible FC chassis and broken up in a scrapyard in Walsall. On 29 March 1937 only the roof and the body framework remained. The bus had been demonstrated to Birmingham between 16 December 1929 and New Year's Eve 1933, and was one of the first double-deckers to be fitted with a very early Gardner 6LW engine. Its chassis went back to Guy Motors and its Gardner 6LW engine was fitted into a new Guy Arab FD chassis that became BCT's 208 (OC 8208). (D. R. Harvey Collection)

249 (OX 1515)
Opposite above: Standing in Cunliffe's yard, Wellington Road, Handsworth Wood, on 24 January 1943, and having been there since June 1935, is 249 (OX 1515). This ADC 507 had entered service on 26 September 1927 and after having been dumped at this site for a period of eight years, its wooden-framed Short H26/26RO had withstood the ravishes of time remarkably well. It is parked alongside the AEC 504 chassis of 146 (OM 9560), while on the left is 257 (OX 1523), another Short-bodied ADC 507. Behind it is 262 (OX 1538), an ADC 507 but with a Birmingham-built John Buckingham H26/26RO body. (L. W. Perkins)

257 (OX 1523)
Oppositw below: Entering service on 27 October 1927, 257 (OX 1523) was still complete in Cunliffe's yard in Handsworth Wood on 24 January 1943. With it and still complete are two other ADC 507s, 249 (OX 1515) and 262 (OX 1538), with a Buckingham body. Thomas Cunliffe was a heavy haulage contractor based at 45 Wellington Road, Handsworth Wood, who had numerous plots of land in the area where he stored vehicles. Cunliffe's bought some twenty-nine assorted AEC 504s and ADC 507s and six single-deck Guy Conquest C single-deckers in June 1935, and over many years broke them up. This was the only time that they bought buses from Birmingham Corporation, though a few vehicles outlasted the company. (L. W. Perkins)

2

Wartime Disposals of 1930s Stock

368 (OF 8368)
Parked in Western Road dump in 1945 is 368 (OF 8368). This was a very early AEC Regent 661 with the chassis number 661035. Delivered in January 1930, it was new as a Short Brothers demonstrator to Birmingham and was originally numbered 96. It had a metal-framed body built by Short and was built as a package deal with the metal-framed Short-bodied lightweight tram 842 of November 1929. 368 was known as 'The Showboat' and had echoes of the tram body with its radiused side windows and the three windows at the rear of the upper saloon. It was withdrawn on 31 July 1944 and was scrapped by Devey of Shenstone in 1946. It is seen here parked between 515 (OC 515) and 513 (OC 513), both of which had been stored since 1943. (D. R. Harvey Collection)

209 (OG 209)

Right: 209 (OG 209), an AEC Regent 661, was a historically important vehicle. It was delivered on 11 November 1930 and had a prototype MCCW H27/21R all-metal body, which had the body contract number 2. It had been tested at Metro-Cammell by shunting a railway wagon into it, which it survived with minor damage. During 1944 it was briefly converted to run on producer gas, but by the time of its withdrawal on 19 September 1945 it had been converted back to petrol. It is parked in Western Road dump near to Dudley Road Hospital after withdrawal in 1945, but, like the Morris-Commercial 538 (OC 538) next to it, it would go back to Elmdon as a non-PSV staff bus for Metro-Cammell. (R. A. Mills)

369 (OG 369)

Below: Awaiting collection at Holford Drive in 1950 by AMCC, an East London second-hand bus dealer whose operating arm was Lansdowne Coaches, are three buses, all withdrawn at the end of January 1950. 369 (OG 369) and 379 (OG 379), AEC Regent 661, originally with English Electric 'piano-front' style bodywork, entered service in August and September 1930 respectively, and in October 1943 were both rebodied with MoS specification Brush H30/21R bodies. On the right is 240 (EOG 240), one of the eighty-five Metro-Cammell-bodied Leyland Titan TD6c's bought for the West Bromwich tramway conversion on 2 April 1939. 240 had entered service on 1 February 1939 and thus was only eleven years old when withdrawn. (D. A. Jones)

383 (OG 383)
Still in BCT's all-over grey livery, 383 (OG 383), another AEC Regent 661 with English Electric 'piano-front' H27/21R bodywork, entered service on 1 October 1930 and was withdrawn on 30 June 1945. It was then sold in March 1946 to Don Everall Ltd (dealer), Wolverhampton service 3/46, who ran it in this condition in their contract fleet as fleet number D8 until it was taken out of service in October 1948. In this condition it looks like the end of the road for 383; however, the clue is in the chassis in front of it. 383 would be stripped down and rebodied with a Burlingham C33F, issued with new chassis number E46/0/48 and re-registered GJW 140, before returning to service 3/49. It was eventually sold for scrap in July 1959. (E. Chitham)

444 (OV 4444)
Above: Awaiting its final dismantling, the engineless 444 (OV 4444) sits in the clay at the bottom of the quarry where Bird's dumped their acquired vehicles before they were broken up. This AEC Regent 661, built in August 1931, was the first of forty fitted with Short H27/21R bodywork and was an early withdrawal on 31 May 1944. It was converted to Service Vehicle 9 as a lorry and arrived at Bird's in March 1954, languishing there until June 1956. (P. Tizard)

396 (OG 396)
Opposite below: The engineless remains of 396 (OG 396) stand in the yard of Devey's of Shenstone, who bought a large number of these petrol-engined AEC Regent 661s and Morris Commercial Imperial double-deckers towards the end of the Second World War. 396 entered service on 1 November 1930 and had an English Electric H27/21R 'piano-front' styled body. It led a fairly uneventful life and, had it not been for the Second World War, most of the class would have been withdrawn by 1939. As it was, of the forty members of the class, nine had been withdrawn by 1938, but with the expectation of war the remainder were kept in service. By 1944, fifteen of the class had been rebodied with new MoS-style Brush bodywork, leaving only sixteen in original condition, which were quickly earmarked for early withdrawal. 396 went on 31 August 1944 and was sold to Devey in May 1946 and broken up. (C. Routh)

469 (OV 4469)

469 (OV 4469) looks very much the worse for wear dumped in Holford Drive in August 1950. Yet, despite its condition, 469 was destined to be one of the longest lived of the pre-war BCT petrol-engined AEC Regent 661s. Originally it had a Short Brothers H27/21R body and was loaned to London Passenger Transport Board, operating from Putney Garage from 29 October to 23 November 1940. On its return it was rebodied with a Brush MoS specification H30/21R in February 1944. OV 4469 was sold to Bird's Commercial Motors Ltd, Stratford-upon-Avon, in January 1951 and was one of fifteen former BCT AECs sold to the High Level Road Bus Co., Nugegoda, Ceylon. It was re-registered IC 1132 in February 1952 and was eventually withdrawn by the Ceylon Transport Board, Colombo, in July 1963. (D. Barlow)

484 (OV 4484)

Opposite above: After a long and interesting career, 484 (OV 4484), an AEC Regent 661 with the first metal-framed production Metro-Cammell body supplied to BCT on 3 December 1931, is an early occupier of Holford Drive, a site recently acquired from the Salvage Department. This bus was loaned to London Transport between 29 October and 22 November 1940 and operated from Holloway Garage. After the massive air raid on Birmingham on the night of 22 November 1940, when Hockley Garage was bombed and a large number of buses were either destroyed or severely damaged, 484 returned to the city. 484 was painted grey in 1942 and ran on producer gas from December 1942 until September 1944. Withdrawn on 31 October 1947, 484 was eventually sold to Don Everall and some of the chassis components were used in their single-decker rebuilding programme. (R. A. Mills)

486 (OV 4486)

Opposite below: 486 (OV 4486) was one of twenty AEC Regent 661s and this bus was delivered to BCT on 4 December 1931. These were among the first buses to be bodied with metal frames by MCCW, with this batch being contract number 5. When new, 486 had acted as an AEC demonstrator when it went to Westcliffe-on-Sea before delivery to Birmingham. It was also one of the thirty Regents sent on loan to London Transport at the outset of the Blitz on the capital. 486 went to London Passenger Transport Board (LPTB) on 30 October 1940 but was returned on 23 November after the heavy air raid on Birmingham. Withdrawn on 30 April 1944, 486 (OV 4486) was sold to Devey of Shenstone in May 1946 and became a static caravan at Sollars Hope, Herefordshire. It was bought for preservation in March 1970 by the 1685 Group before eventually passing to BAMMOT in 1977. In 2015, work began on an extensive and costly restoration, which, when completed, will result in a magnificently preserved bus. (D. R. Harvey Collection)

Wartime Disposals of 1930s Stock

487 (OV 4487)
Above: Dumped in Don Everall's yard off Bilston Road, Wolverhampton, in 1948 are six former Birmingham City Transport AEC Regents, of which four are still in BCT fleet livery. All had been sold to Everall's and their chassis and mechanical units were used in Everall's single-deck rebuilds. 487 (OV 4487), a metal-framed Metro-Cammell-bodied bus on the extreme right, is parked alongside similarly bodied 488 (OV 4488) and 484 (OV 4484), while the grey-painted bus on the right is 365 (OF 3997), fitted with a Brush H26/24R body. (E. Chitham)

OC –
Opposite above: This unidentified Morris-Commercial Imperial HD had a MCCW H28/22R body and was one of forty-seven of this rare petrol-engined marque of double-decker delivered between September and November 1933 to Birmingham Corporation. It was dumped in the undergrowth in a scrapyard near Newbury without any running units and with the front of the bus plated over. The upper saloon was more or less intact but the middle of the lower saloon had largely collapsed. (D. R. Harvey)

528 (OC 528)
Opposite below: Beginning to be stripped of useful spare parts, already withdrawn 528 (OC 528) is at the end of its working life of three years with Mountain Transport (London SW3) in the summer of 1952. This class of forty-seven buses was the largest single batch of Morris-Commercial Imperial HDs to be constructed and its intermediate design of MCCW bodywork was only produced for BCT on these buses, the Guy Arab 208 (OC 8208), the 17–66 batch of Leyland TTBD2 trolleybuses, and, while this metal-framed design was to have a great influence on future Birmingham half-cab orders, the chassis was not very robust. The buses gave a painfully rough ride and rolled a lot. Although the 7.698-litre petrol engine had a good turn of speed, it tended to require constant retuning and had a short crankcase life. The brake pads wore out very quickly and they had very awkward gearboxes. Many of these buses were placed in store at the beginning of the war but thirty-five, including 528, lasted until at least 1945. Many of the forty-seven were sold to Devey of Shenstone, who managed to sell twelve of them for further use, including Mountain Transport (London SW1), who, with the known chassis and engine problems, was very brave and bought six! (A. B. Cross)

Wartime Disposals of 1930s Stock

531 (OC 531)
Above: The batch of Metro-Cammell Morris-Commercial Imperials were bought as an attempt to support local Birmingham industry, but were not long-lived due to the unreliability of the Morris petrol engine, poor steering and a somewhat lightweight chassis. One of the last to be withdrawn was 531 (OC 531), which, after being taken out of service on 30 June 1945, was stored for eleven months before being sold to Devey, a dealer of Shenstone. Sometime later, stripped of its engine, it was used for a number of years as a roadside tea bar along the A449, near the Stewponey Inn, Kinver. (R. G. Grosvenor)

92 (MV 489)
Below: One of only two AEC Renown 663s not to be operated by London General and later London Transport, 92 (MV 489) arrived in Birmingham as an AEC demonstrator in October 1931. This elegant six-wheeler was fitted with a Brush H33/25R body and was purchased in December 1932. It was operated from Harborne Garage but was withdrawn in January 1938, whereupon it emerged the following month as Number 15 in the service fleet. It was fitted with a large crane and was used as a recovery vehicle until September 1961, its moment of glory coming on 4 July 1953 when it was available for pushing trams into the downhill stretch of Carrs Lane where the tram overhead had been removed as they were driven to Kyotts Lake Road Works for breaking up. It was sold to Midland Motors in Golden Hillock Road, Small Heath, in January 1962, outside whose premises it is seen parked awaiting scrapping. (D. Williams)

3

Early Withdrawals of Pre-War Buses

599 (AOG 599)
Holford Drive was first used in 1947 as a parking space for withdrawn buses. This large area was located off Aldridge Road, opposite the Alexander Stadium, and had previously been used by the City Salvage Department. With the impending closure of the tram and trolleybus system, and the parallel decision to get rid of nearly all the pre-war bus stock and all the wartime deliveries, a start was made on withdrawing the fleet more or less chronologically over a seven-year period, starting with the 'piano-front' AEC Regents, the remaining Morris-Commercial Imperials and then the early Daimler COG5s. Three of the early arrivals were 599 (AOG 599), 632 (AOG 632) and the dumped body of 605 (AOG 605), whose chassis had been sold to Don Everall of Wolverhampton. All these buses had entered service in 1934 with MCCW bodywork, and 599 and 632 were sold to Woodfield & Turner in Burnley for scrap. (J. Cull)

617 (AOG 617)
Above: Metro-Cammell-bodied Daimler COG5 617 (AOG 617) entered service on 1 December 1934 and, after being fitted with the similar body from 721 (AOP 721) in June 1944, it was withdrawn in April 1948. But its 'afterlife' was much more interesting as it was used by BCT as a recovery turn-over training vehicle from 17 June 1948 in grey livery at Holford Drive for about three years. The engineless bus is standing abandoned in Holford Drive in July 1954 and was not sold for scrap to Bird's of Stratford until February 1961! (P. Tizard)

641 (AOG 641)
Opposite above: After the destruction of sixty-six trams in the Green Lane depot fire on 7 November 1947, Liverpool Passenger Transport tried to hire twenty Daimler COG5s from Birmingham City Transport but eventually had to purchase them for £350 each, which was really quite extortionate as they were in a very poor state. 641 (AOG 641) entered service as Liverpool's D501 in January 1948 and was withdrawn the following December. It was one of the sixteen bought by Liverpool with somewhat less than robust BRCW bodies, the remaining four having MCCW bodywork. After withdrawal the twenty Daimlers were sold as quickly as possible to a dealer based in Whitchurch in January 1950, who promptly sold them on to Bird's in Stratford for scrap. Three months later it is seen dumped in Bird's yard along with several others, including 670 (AOG 670) alongside it, which had briefly been Liverpool D505. (K. Moody)

672 (AOG 672)
Opposite below: Although it looks as though 672 (AOG 672) is just another bus being broken up at Bird's scrapyard, it is in fact only the BRCW body that is being scrapped. The Daimler COG5 chassis, although withdrawn in 31 January 1946, became Service Vehicle 6 in February 1947 and was used as the Transport Department's pole-painting lorry – a position it held until January 1953. With the imminent abandonment of the Corporation's tram system, the lorry was transferred to Birmingham's Public Works Department and used for streetlamp maintenance and painting. Another chassis-less BRCW lies on its side next to the body of 672. (K. Moody)

Early Withdrawals of Pre-War Buses 25

622 (AOG 622)

Although many of the windows are boarded up, 622 (AOG 622) was one of the handful of buses sold to Used Units of Burnley to be sold on. This Daimler COG5 had a Metro-Cammell body and entered service on 7 December 1934. After withdrawal on 23 November 1947 it went to Yeoman in June 1948 and is seen here dumped at Canon Pyon after withdrawal in June 1950. Despite being sold nearly three years earlier, it still carries the pre-war styled fleet number 622 on the rear panel. (D. R. Harvey Collection)

675 (AOG 675)

Northern Counties were only awarded one contract to build buses for Birmingham and fifteen Daimler COG5s, numbered 674–688. They made a good attempt to replicate the BCT specifications but could always be identified by the thick upper-saloon front corner pillars and the rounded apron above the registration number plate. The bodies were not very robust and withdrawals began around late 1945. 675 (AOG 675) was taken out of service on 31 November 1947 and removed to Holford Drive, where it is seen standing looking very grubby. It was bought by Woodfield & Turner, Burnley, who traded as Used Units, on 31 May 1948. Once a bus was sold to them it was almost inevitably broken up. (A. D. Broughall)

684 (AOG 684)

Withdrawn at the rear of Lea Hall Garage in 1973 is 684 (AOG 684). Like many of the Northern Counties-bodied Daimler COG5s of 1935, this was one of eight transferred to the service fleet, going as number 44 after its conversion to a lorry with a body built behind the original bus cab by Eagle. In this form it had a long life and was transferred to WMPTE on 1 October 1969 and was finally withdrawn in April 1973. (D. R. Harvey Collection)

787 (AOP 787)

With the earlier BRCW body formerly on 639 (AOG 639), Daimler COG5 787 (AOP 787) stands in Woodfield & Turners yard in Burnley in 1949 waiting to be broken up. It had been stored at the British Industries Fair site in Castle Bromwich along with several others since its withdrawal on the last day of May 1948 and was only collected by Used Units in February 1949. Somewhat surprisingly, someone has put the starting handle into the bus. Without a rope though, starting the Gardner 5LW engine would have been difficult! (B. W. Ware Collection)

38 (BOL 38)

Above: The view of Holford Drive in 1951 shows at least six Daimler COG5 single-deckers awaiting collection by Bird's, who bought them on 17 January 1951 and subsequently sold all of them for further service. The complete pre-war Daimler COG5 fleet of single-deckers were all taken out of service when most of the 2231–2260 class of Weymann-bodied Leyland Tiger PS2/1s were delivered between June and 1 October 1950. The odd bus out in the line-up is 38 (BOL 38), which entered service on 1 March 1936, whereas all the others entered service between May and July 1935. The second bus is 66 (AOP 66), which is the only Strachan-bodied bus – all the rest had Metro-Cammell B34F bodywork. Of the rest 61 (AOP 61), which still has its wartime camouflaged roof, while further along the line are 43, 44 and 56, all with AOP registrations. The double-decker, 811 (BOP 811), was not as fortunate as the single-deckers as it too went to Bird's but was broken up. (D. R. Harvey Collection)

39 (BOL 39)

Opposite above: Parked in Holford Drive and looking in very good condition, 39 (BOL 39) is one of the ten Daimler COG5 single-deckers with MCCW bodywork that entered service in March 1936. It was withdrawn on 31 May 1950 and was collected by Bird's in August 1950, who subsequently sold it to an Edinburgh contractor. Alongside it is 34 (BOP 34), which was not as fortunate as it was broken up by Bird's, making it the only one of the ten not to be sold. (R. A. Mills)

94 (BOP 94)

Opposite below: Standing in Bird's quarry, still intact but about to be broken up, is 94 (BOP 94), BCT's only forward entrance bus. This Daimler COG5 was exhibited at the 1935 Commercial Motor Show and was demonstrated to BCT from 27 August 1936 as a comparison to Midland Red's SOS FEDD double-deckers, which had the same front entrance layout. It was purchased on 30 November that year. 94 had a MCCW H28/24F body and it spent all of its fourteen-year working life at Acocks Green Garage, operating on the 1A service. It was sold to Bird's in January 1951 after standing for a few months in Holford Drive. (D. Barlow)

Early Withdrawals of Pre-War Buses

4

Later Withdrawals of Pre-War Buses

814 (BOP 814)
This was the second and final time that Daimler COG5 814 (BOP 814) lay on its side. Originally fitted with a BRCW body, it entered service on 16 September 1936. Allocated to Highgate Road Garage, it was parked next to those premises when it was blown on its side in Queen Street during an air raid on 20 November 1940, being withdrawn ten days later. It was the second bus to be rebodied with ex-Manchester EEC H28/26R's body, which was undertaken by MCCW. It was back in service on 1 January 1942 and was de-licensed and put into the reserve fleet from 31 May 1954 until 1 June 1958. It became one of forty-one COGs to be returned to service, being finally withdrawn on New Year's Eve 1960. 814 was finally bought for scrapping by Bird's in December 1961 and suffered a slow, lingering breaking-up period before finishing up once more on its side sans roof, sans engine, sans almost everything! (D. R. Harvey Collection)

Later Withdrawals of Pre-War Buses

31

862 (BOP 862)
Above: With its fleet number painted out, 862 (BOP 862) has joined 643 (AOG 643) with 'CARR LANE EAST' showing in the destination blind, which has recently returned from its brief sojourn in Liverpool as their D502. 732 (AOP 732) and 132 (EOG 132) are also dumped in Bird's scrapyard in early 1950. All these buses had been purchased by Liverpool Corporation after the disastrous Green Lane depot fire in 1947. With the exception of BRCW-bodied 643, all the buses have MCCW H30/24R bodies and all will be quickly broken up. (A. D. Broughall)

864 (BOP 864)
Below: Despite looking in good order, 864 (BOP 864) – a July 1936-vintage Daimler COG5 with a MCCW H30/24R body – would be shortly taken to Bird's in Stratford on 17 January 1951 and be broken up. Parked alongside it is Park Royal-bodied Guy Arab II 1450 (FOP 450). This also went to Bird's but was sold on to Don Everall of Wolverhampton, where, after being fitted with platform doors, it continued in service in their contract fleet until October 1958. Just visible is 341 (OF 3973), a Brush wartime-rebodied AEC petrol-engined Regent 661 that was also destined for Bird's, but which was broken up. (P. Edgington)

892 (BOP 892)
Above: A line of Metro-Cammell-bodied Daimler COG5s stand in Holford Drive in 1949. This photograph was taken by Kallis Lefkaritis, who, five years later, would return to buy twenty Birmingham double-deckers and export them to Cyprus. The nearest bus is 892 (BOP 892) a 1936 Daimler COG5 with a MCCW body. This would be sold to Midland Motors in Small Heath on 1 February 1950, as would the third bus, 1068 (CVP 168). Both buses would be quickly sold on and scrapped elsewhere before the end of 1950. The second bus is 974 (COX 974), which entered service on 1 May 1937 and was withdrawn after only twelve years' service, being sold for scrap to Bird's on 13 March 1950. (K. Lefkaritis)

905 (COH 905)
Opposite above: Parked in Holford Drive in July 1954 is 905 (COH 905). Entering service in November 1936, this MCCW-bodied Daimler COG5 was withdrawn on New Year's Eve 1952 after it was de-licensed. Some of the primrose paint has been roughly painted over as though its sale was imminent, yet the legal lettering, contrary to normal BCT practice, has not been painted out and there is a chalked 'NOT FOR SALE' notice in the window. Two months later it was collected by Bird's, who immediately sold it to AWRE, Aldermaston, as a staff bus, where it was painted in an unrelieved battleship grey livery. (P. Tizard)

907 (COH 907)
Opposite below: Unceremoniously dumped in their yard, Daimler COG5 907 (COH 907) is in Midland Motors yard with 1346 (FOP 346), a 1944 Weymann-bodied Guy Arab II, in the distance. 907, dating from December 1936, had received a 1937-built Metro-Cammell body (ex-1083) in October 1943; however, although it passed through the hands of three further bus dealers in the search for a buyer, it was broken up by Grice, West Bromwich, in June 1951. (D. R. Harvey Collection)

Later Withdrawals of Pre-War Buses

910 (COH 910)
Above: The vast wasteland of Holford Drive can be appreciated, though by 1954 its days of storing withdrawn BCT buses was largely over as the sale of withdrawn buses had finally been achieved. Late arrivals were 910 (COH 910), a Metro-Cammell-bodied Daimler COG5 dating from December 1936, and, behind it, 1163 (FOF 163), a similar combination of chassis and body but dating from August 1939 and with a slightly upgraded body, without guttering over the upper-saloon front windows. It would be sold to Bird in October 1954 and then to Elms Coaches of Kenton, whereas 910 would briefly become a snowplough before being sold via Bird's to Lloyd's, Nuneaton. In the background, standing on its own, is the grey-painted hulk of turn-over bus 617 (AOG 617). (A. B. Cross)

971 (COX 971)
Opposite above: A brick-built site hut was built next to the entrance to Holford Drive, which was equipped with a water supply and a stove with a readily available wheelbarrow full of coke. The hut was used by the men employed to guard the site and to record the movement of buses both in and out. They also had time to construct a small rockery garden. Parked with stone chocks in front of both tyres is 971 (COX 971), a 1937 Daimler COG5 with a Samlesbury Engineering renovated body originally mounted on 895 (COH 895). Although withdrawn at the end of September 1952, it would remain at Holford Drive for some time as it was purchased by Bird's in March 1954, who promptly broke it up. Identifiable in the background is the severely accident-damaged 'unfrozen' Leyland-bodied Leyland Titan TD7 1329 (FON 629). (L. Deakin)

978 (COX 978)
Opposite below: After being withdrawn on New Year's Eve 1960 and sold to Bird's, 978 (COX 978) was used for three months by Cardiff coach operator Raymond Prance, who even had time to put his own advertisements on the bus. 978 eventually found its way to the Cardiff scrapyard of W. A. Way, who had acquired the bus in November 1961. It had been fitted with an English Electric H28/24R body in mid-March 1949. This streamline body was one of twenty purchased from Manchester in 1941 and had initially been fitted to BOP 842 in March 1942. (J. Carroll)

Later Withdrawals of Pre-War Buses 35

1005 (CVP 105)

Above: Parked in Holford Drive in July 1954 is 1005 (CVP 105), with 1057 (CVP 157) behind it. Both these Daimler COG5s had MCCW H30/24R bodies and dated from July and late August 1937. 1057 was put into the reserve fleet and returned to service on 1 May 1958, while on 1 November 1954, despite its good condition, it was selected to be one of twenty-four COG5s to become snowploughs, which were added to another ten that were converted in 1953. The buses had their life rails removed and a diagonally set blade was fitted so that any snow would be cleared and pushed towards the gutter as the bus moved along. Each garage had at least one snowplough and they were started up every six weeks or so, but frequently the buses were not used from one year to the next as they only ventured out on the rare occasion when the main roads needed to be cleared of snow. Nearly all these pre-war buses were withdrawn on 31 July 1963 and they were sold to Nutton's of Barnsley by auction on 2 September 1963. (P. Tizard)

1015 (CVP 115)

Opposite above: 1950 was one of the peak years for Holford Drive being used. A concerted effort was made to make large inroads into the pre-war fleet of Daimler COG5 double- and single-deckers and the Metro-Cammell-bodied Leyland Titan TD6cs, and, unlike the following four years, the vast majority of the double-deckers were sold for scrap. Daimler COG5 1015 (CVP 115) had a MCCW H30/24R body and was new on 1 July 1937. To the left is 283 (EOG 283), a Leyland Titan TD6c with a Metro-Cammell H28/24R that entered service on 25 March 1939, just a week before the West Bromwich tramway conversion, and, like 1015, was withdrawn on 31 May 1950. Both buses were sold to Bird's Commercial Motors – 1015 on 17 January 1951 and 283 on 26 September 1950 – and were broken up. The Strachan-bodied single-deck Daimler COG5, 70 (AOP 70), was sold to Stevenson, Spath, in early 1951 and ran with them until March 1960. (P. Tizard)

1024 (CVP 124)

Opposite below: This ignominious end was what awaited most BCT buses, especially if they went to Bird's Commercial Motors in Stratford. The denuded framework of 1937-built MCCW-bodied Daimler COG5 1024 (CVP 124) has been pitched down the steep slope into the bottom of the former quarry and has its nose buried in the platform of the overturned English Electric rebodied 814 (BOP 814). Both buses were among the last of the forty-one pre-war Daimler's to be returned to service in 1958, when the Walsall Road and New Oscott routes were transferred from Midland Red. Both were taken out of service on 31 December 1960. (A. D. Broughall)

Later Withdrawals of Pre-War Buses

1036 (CVP 136)

Above: In 1937, BCT bought five Leyland-bodied Leyland Titan TD4cs and five AEC Regent 661s with virtually standard BCT-style MCCW H30/26R bodies. 1036 (CVP 136) entered service on 1 July 1937 and led a fairly uneventful life at Liverpool Street Garage until it was withdrawn. It is parked up on the Holford Drive lot in Perry Barr with the similar 1035 (CVP 135) behind it and Daimler COG5 164 (EOG 164), with a BRCW H30/24R body, that had entered service on 1 December 1938. Both 1036 and 164 had been withdrawn on 30 April 1949, while all three were sold to Bird's on 27 July 1949 and broken up. (S. E. Letts)

1039 (CVP 139)

Below: Looking as though it was ready to be started up and driven out of Bird's scrapyard to a prospective purchaser is 1039 (CVP 139). Alas, by the early 1960s the market for the excellently maintained BCT pre-war Daimler COG5 had all but dried up as vast numbers of redundant former London Transport RTs and RTLs began flooding the second-hand bus market for knock-down prices. 1039 had been withdrawn on 31 December 1960 and was sold on 14 February 1961 and broken up. (A. D. Broughall)

1049 (CVP 149) and 1113 (CVP 213)

Above: Looking in excellent condition, 1049 (CVP 149) and 1113 (CVP 213) are parked in the Bird's quarry below the old brickworks building in the early spring of 1961. The Daimler COG5 1049 had entered service on 1 August 1937 and after being rebodied in July 1948 it was initially withdrawn on 30 September 1954 and placed in reserve fleet, until it was resurrected in September 1957. 1113 was four months newer and like 1049 was taken out of service on 31 December 1960. Within three months both were scrapped. (P. Yeomans)

1052 (CVP 152)

Below: One last spin around the scrapyard! In a cloud of exhaust smoke 1052 (CVP 152) is driven to its own funeral as it is manoeuvred into its last resting place in the quarry at Bird's on 15 April 1961. Within a few days a start would be made to remove the Gardner 5LW engine, tyres and wheels, and the glass. Later, the aluminium body panels would be stripped and within two years the bus would be barely recognisable. (A. N. Porter)

1055 (CVP 155)

Above: Robbed of its running units and back axle, the body of 1055 (CVP 155) had only had a few aluminium panels removed as it sits in the clinging mud in Bird's Stratford-upon-Avon scrapyard in the early spring of 1961. Entering service on 17 August 1937, this MCCW-bodied Daimler COG5 retained its original body throughout its long career, albeit renovated by Samlesbury Engineering during March 1948. After being placed in the reserve fleet, the bus returned to service for just over two years at Moseley Road Garage until it was withdrawn on New Year's Eve 1959. (D. R. Harvey Collection)

1069 (CVP169)

Opposite above: Once despatched into Bird's quarry, hardly any bus ever re-emerged, yet 1069 (CVP 169) did, although the new owner was never recorded. This Daimler COG5, of October 1937 vintage, was among the last to be withdrawn after a long career that ended on 31 December 1960, though for the previous seven months it had been de-licensed. Behind it is 1008 (CVP 108), one of only two of the Daimler COG5s fitted out as a snowplough in November 1954 to be sold for scrap on 31 May 1960. On the right is the still intact Manchester-style English Electric-bodied 814 (BOP 814). (A. D. Broughall)

1079 (CVP 179)

Opposite below: Only a dozen of the 100 CVP-registered Daimler COG5s of 1937 were withdrawn in 1949 and 1079 (CVP 179) was one of these. It was bought by Bird's in December 1949 and was immediately broken up. It had been rebodied with a similar Metro-Cammell body at the end of August 1946 and stands surrounded by the detritus of previously broken-up vehicles. In the distance, beneath the chimney of the former brickworks, are some even earlier BCT buses to arrive at the Stratford-upon-Avon scrapyard. (D. R. Harvey Collection)

Later Withdrawals of Pre-War Buses

1084 (CVP 184), 1107 (CVP 207)

Above: The 'top shed' alongside Birmingham Road in Stratford-upon-Avon was where buses being offered for sale, rather than selected for scrapping, were parked. Daimler COG5 1084 (CVP 184) had been bought by Bird on 14 February 1961 but after hanging around undercover for about a year, it was unable to find a buyer and was subsequently scrapped. Alongside it, 1107 (CVP 207) was more fortunate, being bought for preservation in July 1964 by Barry Ware and in November 2017 it celebrated its 80th birthday. It was rebodied twice, the second time receiving a later 1939 MCCW body from 1216 (FOF 216) in December 1950, which lacked the rain shield over the front upper-saloon windows. (E. Surfleet)

1139 (DON 439)

Below: How the mighty have fallen! 1139 (DON 439) was exhibited at the 1937 Commercial Motor Show and was originally intended to have been registered EOG 101. It was rebodied with the 1937 MCCW H30/24R body transferred from Daimler COG5 (CVP 228) on 30 November 1948. It has been reduced to a skeletal frame inside the former brickworks in 1956. The bus next to it unidentifiable but the third vehicle is 239 (EOG 239), a MCCW-bodied Leyland Titan TD6c, which had returned to Bird's from J. Laurie of Hamilton, where it had been used between 1953 and 1956. (P. Tizard)

128 (EOG 128)

Above: On the left, reduced to a single-decker, is 1938 Daimler COG5 128 (EOG 128). On the right is the unidentifiable remains of an ex-BCT Manchester-style English Electric body. Both buses were acquired via Bird's in 1955 and were quickly reduced to a B28F layout; in this state they lasted in service for around three to six years. They are in the Larnaca scrapyard of Lefkaritis, who operated a large fleet of second-hand buses along the south coast of Cyprus, taking in Limassol and the British military base at Akrotiri. All the buses were dumped in the Larnaca yard, but were engulfed by a fire that got out of control in 1981. Lefkaritis also supplied most of the oil and petrol on the Mediterranean island of Cyprus with the brand name Petrolina, operated a fleet of oil tanker ships and owned an airline. (J. Dovey)

151 (EOG 151), 226 (EOG 226)

Below: In the mid-1950s the waste ground next to Washwood Heath Garage began to be used to park up withdrawn buses before they were sold to Bird's. On 18 March 1954, 151 (EOG 151) was the first of the 1938 batch BRCW-bodied Daimler COG5s and entered service on 6 October of that year but swapped its body for the MCCW body formerly on 924 (COH 924). The bus nearest to the garage wall is 226 (EOG 226), a Leyland Titan TD6c with a torque convertor gearbox and the later style of MCCW body without the rain shield over the front upper-saloon windows. The Leyland was sold to Lloyds of Nuneaton, who ran it for just over two years, while the Daimler was last seen in a Westcliff-on-Sea scrapyard in 1955. They are both delicensed in the garage yard on 18 March 1954. (D. S. Giles)

154 (EOG 154)
Above: Dumped in Ashmore's scrapyard in West Bromwich is a very careworn 154 (EOG 154). This Daimler COG5 has a BRCW H30/24R body, which, except for being painted grey in 1942, had not had much modified since it entered service on 1 November 1938. Just over eleven years later it was sold for scrap: this was in part because the quality of the construction of the BRCW bodies was not as good as their Metro-Cammell contemporaries. (D. R. Harvey Collection)

166 (EOG 166)
Below: On 9 August 1987 the remains of 166 (EOG 166) stands in the blazing heat in the Larnaca scrapyard of Lefkaritis in Larnaca, Cyprus. Amazingly, the Gardner 5LW engine is still in the Daimler COG5 chassis. As Cypriot-registered TL 284 it ran as a single-decker for about three years from September 1954 before being dumped in Lefkaritis' yard. The top deck was used as a beach hut on the Famagusta coastline before being destroyed during the Turkish invasion of Cyprus in 1974. (D. R. Harvey)

213 (EOG 213)
Above: There was not much left of 213 (EOG 213) as it lay on its side in Bird's scrapyard after it had been returned from J. Laurie of Hamilton. It had arrived in Stratford-upon-Avon in June 1956. This MCCW-bodied Leyland Titan TD6c was one of just five of the class of eighty-five tramway replacement buses that had entered service in December 1938, initially being allocated to Acocks Green Garage but moving to Hockley Garage on 2 April 1939 after nearly all the tramcars had been transferred to other depots around the city. 213 was one of the five buses in this class that exchanged bodies, receiving the body from 253 (EOG 253) on 1 February 1949. (J. Fozard)

220 (EOG 220)
Below: 220 (EOG 220) was one of the unfortunate Leyland Titan TD6cs to be withdrawn early and immediately broken up. Entering service in January 1939 and used exclusively after 2 April 1939 on the tram at replacement services to West Bromwich, Wednesbury and Dudley, 220 was withdrawn on 31 January 1950 and scrapped by the end of the year. It is standing, already minus its headlights, awaiting the first bites of Bird's cutters torch. (D. Barlow)

267 (EOG 267)

Above: Prior to being advertised for sale, many pre-war buses had their cream livery areas roughly painted over in blue. 267 (EOG 267), a MCCW-bodied Leyland Titan TD6c, entered service on 8 March 1939 and was taken out of service on 30 November 1950 before being sold to Bird's in early June 1951. Behind it, resting on its axles, are two Birmingham trolleybuses, including six-wheeler Leyland TTBD2 63 (OC 1163) and 69 (COX 69), a 1937-built Leyland TB5 with a MCCW H29/24R body, which has already been stripped of its roof. (K. Moody)

284 (EOG 284)

Below: This still is taken from the film *The Long Arm*, released in June 1956. The film had the distinction of being the last Ealing Film to be made at Borehamwood Studios. It starred Jack Hawkins as Supt Tom Halliday, who is investigating a series of safe-breaking robberies. In the last robbery the getaway car hits a bystander, who manages to pass limited information to the police before dying. The hit-and-run vehicle is found in a scrapyard, which also contains ex-Birmingham bus 284 (EOG 284). This Leyland Titan TD6c with a MCCW H28/24R body was taken out of service on 31 January 1950, and after being used by Lansdowne Luxury Coaches in East London, it briefly became a film star in a scrapyard! (D. R. Harvey Collection)

Later Withdrawals of Pre-War Buses

1156 (FOF 156)
Above: With over 6¾ tons precariously standing on bricks, 1156 (FOF 156) stands without wheels or tyres in Holford Drive in July 1954. Two months later it was sold to Bird's and exported to Cyprus, where it ran as a single-decker until January 1958. These FOF-registered Daimler COG5s had the final pre-war BCT styled Metro-Cammell body modifications, with deeper platform and upper-saloon rear windows and a lack of a rain shield above the upper-saloon front windows. This bus had entered service on 1 August 1939 and was taken out of service on 30 April 1954, by this point carrying the body formerly on 1149 (FOF 149). (P. Tizard)

1241 (FOF 241)
Below: The last batch of pre-war Daimler COG5s numbered thirty buses and were bodied by Birmingham Railway Carriage & Wagon Company (BRCW), based in Handsworth. The BRCW bodies were not as robust as their MCCW equivalents and tended to be withdrawn earlier. 1241 (FOF 241) entered service on the Friday before war was declared on Germany. The bus is in Holford Drive but unlike 1000 (CVP 100) and the Leyland-bodied Leyland Titan TD6c next to it, it has, like all the other buses behind it, its cream paintwork roughly painted over with a single coat of blue paint. This was supposed to stop the buses running as second-hand acquisitions in BCT livery. 1241 was sold to Croxley Coaches, who ran it until about 1960. (R. A. Mills)

1238 (FOF 238)

Above: Late arrivals at Holford Drive were Daimler COG5s 1238 (FOF 238) and 1010 (CVP 110), which both arrived in 1954. Both buses would see further service, though in very different circumstances. 1010, with its standard MCCW H30/24R body, has the renovated body formerly on 918 (COH 912), which had been damaged in an air raid on 20 November 1940. It was fitted to 1010 in May 1942 after its original body was burnt out. 1010 became a snowplough in November 1954 and was always parked just inside the entrance doors to Rosebery Street Garage until it was made redundant on 31 July 1963. 1238 (FOF 238) was the only pre-war BCT bus to have a Park Royal body. Entering service well into the Second World War on 1 March 1940, the body was a speculative venture produced as a possible precursor to winning an order. Of course, the wartime closure of the bus industry meant that 1238 was to remain unique and it was withdrawn in July 1951. At first sight it looked like any other pre-war COG5 body but close examination of just the front aspect shows many differences. It must have been stored for over two years before being sold to Bird's, who then exported it to Lefkaritis in Larnaca, Cyprus, in September 1954. (P. Tizard)

1269 (FOF 269)

Opposite above: The very last Daimler COG5 delivered to BCT was 1269 (FOF 269), which entered service on 1 November 1939. It also had the last BRCW body built for the municipality. It was rebodied with the English Electric H28/26R body originally intended for Manchester Corporation on 31 August 1949, which it carried until 31 October 1953, when it was withdrawn. It is parked in Holford Drive in July 1954 before being sold to Bird's in September 1954, whereupon it ran with Lloyds of Nuneaton and Chapel End Coaches until it was finally taken out of service in September 1958. It is parked alongside 1273 (FOF 273), a Leyland Titan TD6c with a Leyland H28/24R body, which was also sold to Lloyd of Nuneaton. (P. Tizard)

1271 (FOF 271), 1276 (FOF 276) and 1317 (FOF 317)

Opposite below: All three of these magnificent-looking late 1939-built Leyland-bodied Leyland Titan TD6cs were withdrawn on 28 February 1954. There were fifty of these buses, which were ordered to replace the Dudley Road trams on 1 October 1939. These three are parked in Holford Drive in the spring of 1954 and because of their excellent condition nearly all of the class of fifty were snapped up very quickly after their initial disposal to Bird's. This trio were sold either to Lloyd of Nuneaton or, in the case of 1276, to Northern Roadways, Glasgow. (P. Tizard)

Later Withdrawals of Pre-War Buses 49

1283 (FOF 283)

Above: Along with 1281, 1283 (FOF 283) was severely damaged during the air raid at Hockley Garage on the night of 22 November 1940. As a result, once extricated from the mangled frames of destroyed bodies, it was withdrawn two days later. The shortage of buses had now become critical and thirty AEC Regents on loan to London Transport were returned, having been in the capital for exactly a month. Once it was realised that the complete top deck from withdrawn buses could be fitted, 1283 and 1281 were both equipped with MCCW top decks transferred from already withdrawn Morris Imperials 553 (OC 553) and 536 (OC 536) respectively. Alas they did not line up with the lower saloon, most noticeably at the front above the cab. Additionally, two Daimler COG5 also received top decks with 912 (COH 912) getting the one from 532 and 927 (COH 927) getting the one from 520. 1283 was reinstated on 25 February 1941 and was withdrawn on 24 March 1949 after receiving terminal nearside body damage in an accident. It is seen parked here in Holford Drive before being sold to Bird's on 27 July 1949. (S. E. Letts)

1294 (FOF 294), 1318 (FOF 318)

Below: 1294 (FOF 294) and 1318 (FOF 318) entered service on 7 September 1939 and 1 November 1939 respectively, but after withdrawal on 30 November 1950 and 1952 they followed a nearly identical 'afterlife'. Both passed to Bird's Commercial Motors, Stratford-upon-Avon, acting as a dealer, and the pair was sold to Lansdowne Luxury Coaches (London E10). After withdrawal they were sold again in January 1955 to Doughty, Kings Lynn, before returning to Bird's for scrapping in April 1958. Both are well on their way to being dismantled when seen in 1958. (PM Photography)

5

Wartime Buses

1322 (FVP 922)
1320–1323 (FVP 920–923) had pre-war specification 8-foot-wide bodies, which were built as part of MCCW contract 239 for five H32/26R bodies mounted on Daimler COG6s chassis. They were part of an order for five similar vehicles intended for Johannesburg Municipality but that could not be shipped due to German U-boat activity in the Atlantic Ocean. The four for Birmingham were delivered at a rate of one per month between December 1941 and March 1942 in wartime grey livery, and were immediately subjected to height and width restrictions and banned from entering the city centre. As a result, they were banished for a number of years to Yardley Wood Garage for use on the outer suburban 18 route. Eventually going to Harborne Garage and later Quinton Garage, they were allowed into the city and worked on the 9 route along the wide and straight Hagley Road to Quinton. All were withdrawn on 30 September 1954 and all four, led by 1322 (FVP 922) along with 1323 (FVP 923) and 1320 (FVP 920) with the older styled front dome, are seen here parked in Holford Drive. All were sold to Bird's just over a week after withdrawal and the four were quickly sold on for further service, with 1322 going to Proctors of Hanley and lasting until 1960. (R. Marshall)

1329 (FON 629)

Above: 1329–1331 (FON 629–631) were the second trio of 'unfrozen' Leyland Titan TD7s built to Leyland's pre-war specification, 1324–1326 (FON 324–326) being the first three. They were originally intended for Western SMT Co. Ltd, Kilmarnock, but were reallocated to Birmingham. 1329 (FON 629) was delivered in a wartime grey livery on 4 July 1942, some five months after the first of the six Leyland-bodied Leylands. They were based at Perry Barr Garage as they operated on the longest routes in Birmingham, which suited their slow gear changes that in normal circumstances would have made driving them hard work. 1329 was the first of the six to be withdrawn after a collision that destroyed most of the cab structure in September 1951, though it hung around at Holford Drive until it was purchased by Bird's in March 1954. (R. Knibbs)

1336 (FOP 336)

Opposite above: Birmingham only received five wartime Guy Arab Is, the penultimate one, 1336 (FOP 336), entering service on 12 November 1942. They were delivered from Weymann in all-over grey livery, with 1336 being the first of the five to be repainted in BCT livery on 9 March 1945 and the last of the quintet to be withdrawn after a very short service life on 31 October 1949. It is seen here in Bird's yard in Stratford, from where it was sold to a showman and cut down to the upper-saloon waistrail and used as a lorry. Next to it is 195 (EOG 195), a BRCW-bodied Daimler Cog5 that entered service on 1 January 1939 and was withdrawn in April 1949, before going to Bird's and broken up. On the right is 246 (EOG 246), a Leyland Titan TD6c with a Metro-Cammell H28/24R body that was five weeks newer than 195. It too was an early withdrawal in October 1949, but spent ten years operating for a number of Scottish independents, the last of whom, Paton Brothers of Renfrew, even rebodied it with a second-hand wartime Alexander L27/26R body. (D. R. Harvey Collection)

1361 (FOP 361)

Opposite below: Awaiting sale in Bird's Stratford scrapyard on 30 April 1951 is 1361 (FOP 361). This Duple-bodied Daimler CWA6 dated from February 1944 and was retired on New Year's Eve 1949 when not quite six years old. The vehicle was exported in October 1951 to the South Western Omnibus Company of Colombo in Ceylon (now Sri Lanka), where it ran until 1960 before being rebodied as a single-decker. It lasted until early 1968 before running as a lorry until about 1981. (A. D. Packer)

Wartime Buses

1345 (FOP 345)

Above: One of the earliest 'utility' Birmingham City Transport buses to be taken out of service was Weymann-bodied Guy Arab II 5LW 1345 (FOP 345), which was withdrawn on 31 January 1949. It had entered service on 8 November 1943 in wartime grey livery and was repainted for the only time in full fleet livery on 23 December 1947, some eighteen months after it had its wooden-slatted seats replaced. It was sold directly to Rowbotham, Harriseahead, in 1949 and by January 1951 was licensed to Leon of Finningley. By 1954 it had been cut down to a lorry and lasted in this form until 1960, thus being used as a second-hand vehicle for twice as long as it was used by BCT. Parked behind 1345 in Holford Drive in June 1950 is an unidentified Duple-bodied Daimler CWA6 and to the left is 892 (BOP 892), a 1936 BRCW-bodied Daimler COG5 withdrawn on 30 November 1949, while on the right is 39 (BOL 39), a single-deck Daimler COG5 with a MCCW B34F body dating from 1 March 1936 that was taken out of service on 31 May 1950. (D. R. Harvey Collection)

1390 (FOP 390)

Below: Lined up in Bird's yard in Stratford are five Daimler CWA6s. They are 1390 (FOP 390) and 1387 (FOP 387), both dating from 25 March 1945 and fitted with Park Royal bodywork. In the middle of the row are Duple-bodied 1453 (FOP 453), dating from New Year's Day 1945, and 1359 (FOP 359), which was new into service exactly one year earlier. The distant bus is 1460 (FOP 460), which was delivered well after the end of the Second World War on 8 October 1945 and was destined to have a service life with Birmingham of only four years and two months. Only 1390 and 1460 ever ran again as PSVs, with the former lasting until March 1960 with Morley of West Row and the latter having three years with Proctor of Hanley. 1453 became a lorry while 1387 and 1359 were broken up by Bird's. (P. Tizard)

1396 (FOP 396)

Converted to dual-control driver-trainer 96 in May 1952 and then converted to a tree lopper in January 1959, 1396 (FOP 396) originally had a Park Royal MoS H30/26R body and was new in March 1944. After being withdrawn it received the second-hand wartime Brush H30/24R body formerly on the September 1930-vintage AEC Regent 661 chassis, 416 (OG 416), which had been withdrawn on 30 April 1938 and converted to a driver-trainer and in 1948 fitted with the Brush body from 398 (OG 398), another Regent. 1396 is in the yard of Wombwell Diesels, having arrived there in the summer of 1970. (PM Photography)

1401 (FOP 401)

Another dual-control trainer was Guy Arab II 5LW 1401 (FOP 401), which was the first of two Guys originally with Strachan bodywork, in this case entering service on 1 February 1945. It became a trainer numbered 93 with the second-hand Brush body from 414 (OG 414) in December 1951 and was not withdrawn until January 1968, when four of the six converted buses were withdrawn. 1401 was sold along with similar conversions 1383 and 1384 to Hartwood Finance in Barnsley, in whose yard it is seen being dismantled just too soon for the preservation movement to buy it. (D. Akrigg)

1407 (FOP 407)
Above: The first of the second batch of Park Royal-bodied Guy Arab II Gardner 7.0-litre 5LW-engined bus was 1407 (FOP 407). It entered service on 10 June 1944 and was taken out of service on 20 July 1950, which, despite its apparent good condition, was about par for wartime bus withdrawals. It is parked awaiting disposal in Holford Drive in 1950. It was sold via Bird's to Don Everall in Wolverhampton, who fitted it with platform doors and ran it until April 1959. The two 1937-built Metro-Cammell-bodied Daimler COG5s are 1015 (CVP 115) and 1064 (CVP 164). Both were sold to Bird's on 17 January 1951, with 1015 being broken up and 1064 running for a Leicestershire showman until 1956. On the extreme left is a March 1939-delivered 275 (EOG 275), a Leyland Titan TD6c with a MCCW body that was taken out of service on 20 July 1950, and which spent just seven months with Thomas Brothers, Port Talbot. (P. Tizard)

1430 (FOP 430)
Left: Parked in Holford Drive, both 1430 (FOP 430), a Duple-bodied Daimler CWA6 of February 1945, and 459 (OV 4459), a wartime Brush-rebodied petrol-engined AEC Regent 661 whose chassis dated from September 1931, look a little past their best, though structurally intact, as they await delivery to Bird's in early 1951. They would both be exported to Ceylon by 1952, with 459 going to the High Level Road Bus Co. in Nugegoda, a suburb of Colombo, and 1430 sold to the South Western O. C. in Colombo. (D. Barlow)

1426 (FOP 426)

Above: 1426 (FOP 426) had recently arrived at the Holford Drive site and still has recent timetable alteration notices in the windows. It stands across the front of single-deck 39 (BOL 39), a 1936 Daimler COG5 with a MCCW B34F body that had been withdrawn at the end of May 1950. The deeply upholstered seats on the upper deck of Duple-bodied Daimler CWA6 1426 had been fitted in December 1947, replacing the original wooden slatted ones. At the same time it had received it's only 'clean and varnish', which was Tyburn Road's phrase for a repaint. The characteristic features of the wartime Duple body were the thin body pillars, the raised bottom of the off-side driver's cab with the angled corner to the top of the driver's door and the 'lobster shell' rear dome. 1426 was withdrawn from service from Liverpool Street Garage on 30 April 1950. On 20 July 1950 it was 'taken off strength for disposal' and a month later was sold to Bird's for disposal, going to Kearsey of Cheltenham in October 1951 and staying in service with them for another nine years. (D. R. Harvey Collection)

1434 (FOP 434)

Below: 1434 (FOP 434) was a Guy Arab II originally with a Park Royal MoS H30/26R body, which entered service on 1 September 1944. After withdrawal on 30 November 1950 its chassis received the 1943 Brush body, which had been fitted to 452 (OV 4452) at the end of 1951. The bus was converted to a dual-control driver-trainer and after being numbered 94 in the service fleet survived until December 1964. It is parked on the waste ground alongside Washwood Heath Garage with Washwood Heath Road in the distance. It is sometime before its collection in March 1965 by Taylor's, a breaker based in Stafford, although 1434 was actually broken up in a yard in Brierley Hill. (A. N. Scott)

1455 (FOP 455)
Awaiting collection from Holford Drive by Bird's in early 1951 are three Guy Arab IIs painted in all-over blue in order to prevent them being seen as a second-hand bus in Birmingham livery. All were taken out of service during 1950. 1455 (FOP 455) had a Park Royal body, while 1371 (FOP 371) had a Weymann body, as did 1350 (FOP 350) on the right. All three were sold by Bird's and all turned up with Murphy, a Leicestershire dealer based in Rearsby village, between Leicester and Melton Mowbray. (D. Barlow)

1477 (FOP 477)
After withdrawal on the last day of January 1951, 1477 (FOP 477), a Park Royal MoS H30/26R-bodied Daimler CWA6D, was taken to Holford Drive prior to disposal; although appearing a little dusty, the bus looks worthy of further service. Parked alongside is 1464 (FOP 464), which was virtually the same except that it had a normal Kirkstall Forge rear axle. Both buses were sold to Kearsey of Cheltenham after passing through the hands of bus dealer W. T. Bird of Stratford-upon-Avon, with 1477 remaining in service until April 1961. (P. Edgington)

6
Trolleybuses Disposals

18 (UK 8341)
A demonstration trolleybus, a Guy-bodied Guy BTX, arrived in Birmingham on 22 February 1930 and stayed for seventeen months until 31 May 1931. Numbered 18, it was registered in Wolverhampton as UK 8341, whereas its twin, a Guy BTX numbered 19, stayed for just one week, and yet perversely was registered in Birmingham as OG 9886. Demonstrator 18 (UK 8341) had a 60 hp Rees-Roturbo compound-wound motor and a Guy H27/26R body. It was returned to Guy Motors in September 1931. It was eventually sold in January 1935 to Llanelly District Electric Supply Co. Ltd as their 17 and reregistered TH 5166. After it was withdrawn in 1945 it was sold to Balfour Beatty in December 1946 and is visible on the right being used as workman's hut at Carmarthen Bay Power Station, Burry Port, until May 1949. (D. R. Harvey Collection)

19 (OV 1175)

Above: The very first Leyland trolleybus to be built was demonstrated to Birmingham City Tramways Department as their trolleybus 19 (OV 1175). It was used on the Nechells route from 20 May 1931 and was returned to Leyland Motors in August 1931. Its only other demonstration duty was briefly on the Chesterfield Corporation system later the same month. After its return to Leyland Motors, the trolleybus languished in the South Works until it was converted to a TD1 petrol-engined chassis and sold to Jersey Motors as 25 (J 1199) in February 1934. Indistinguishable from the other TD1s in the JMT fleet, it survived the German Occupation and was retired in 1958. It was immediately purchased by Colin Shears for preservation at Winkleigh, has been reregistered twice as MJX 222J and later as SV 6107, and is still preserved. 19 has, ironically, the distinction of being the only Birmingham trolleybus to be preserved, albeit as a petrol-engined motor bus. It is seen here parked outside the West of England Collection premises at Winkleigh still in a withdrawn condition some ten years after its purchase for preservation. (B. W. Ware)

1 (OV 4001)

Opposite above: Dumped in Holland's scrapyard in Oldbury are two of the half-cab Leyland TBD1s. The enforced closure of the Nechells trolleybus route on 30 September 1940 put all eleven of these half-cab Leylands, numbered 1–11, off the road, although 4–11 had been stored since the February of that year after the dozen FOK-registered Leyland TB7s were delivered. All five of the AEC 663Ts, numbered 12–16, and the first five of the Leyland TTBD2s were also put into store in Sampson Road paint shop. The vacant storage space in the paint shop had been created in the spring of 1939, when most of the re-painting of the tram fleet was transferred back to Kyotts Lake Road Works. The intention to reintroduce them on the Nechells route was never a realistic proposition and by 1944 a considerable amount of the overhead had been taken down for use elsewhere on the system. The OC-registered Leylands were returned to service in December 1940, but the sixteen earlier trolleybuses never ran again and were sold to Midland Motors of Golden Hillock Road, Small Heath, to be broken up. However, 1 (OV 4001) and 8 (OV4015), as well as AEC 16 (OJ 1016), were sold to Holland's for scrapping and the two Leylands were still there on 9 June 1950. (D. R. Harvey Collection)

17–66 class

Above: By December 1951 the Birmingham trolleybuses were still largely intact and eleven of them are lined up in Bird's yard. They look a little more weather-beaten, but generally seem to be in reasonable condition. Most of the trolleybuses are the six-wheeled 17–66 class but at the far end of the line are two four-wheelers, which are distinguishable by having cream-painted waistrails below the lower-saloon windows. It would be another six months before any effort was made to break up these trolleybuses after negotiations to sell the FOK-registered four-wheelers to Durban in South Africa came to nothing. (D. F. Parker)

28 (OC 1128)

Surrounded in the distance by withdrawn Daimler COG5s and Metro-Cammell-bodied Leyland Titan TD6c, 28 (OC 1128), a MCCW-bodied six-wheeled Leyland TTBD2, still retains its upper-saloon seats, but nearly everything else has gone. This was one of the earliest of the BCT trolleybuses to be broken up as all the external aluminium panels and glass have gone, as has most of its roof as it stands on its tyre-less wheels in Bird's scrapyard in the spring of 1952. (L. Mason)

29 (OC 1129)

The Birmingham blue livery has weathered to a bleached powder blue after eighteen years' exposure to the elements in Bird's scrapyard at Stratford-upon-Avon. Long after all the other Birmingham trolleybuses had been broken up, the remains of the lower saloons of six-wheeled Leyland TTBD2 29 (OC 1129) and Leyland TB7 four-wheeler 73 (COX 73) were still identifiable in 1969, less than a year before the scrapyard site was cleared. Both of these trolleybuses had been taken to Bird's in the spring of 1952, having first gone to Cunliffe's yard in Handsworth. (D. R. Harvey)

37 (OC 1137)

The towing vehicles employed were a variety of ex-Second World War military vehicles. Most common was the AEC Matador, but other vehicles were also used. Pausing for a countryside break on the A34, the leading trolleybus, 37 (OC 1137), is being towed by a Commer Q4 4x2 3-tonner, fitted with a WD body. The second trolleybus is being towed by an ex-US Army Studebaker 6x6 truck. The trolleybuses were towed along the A34 through Solihull and Henley-in-Arden. (J. Whybrow)

41 (OC 1141)
Well underway to being broken up in mid-1952 are two of the 1934 Metro-Cammell Leyland TTBD2s six-wheeled trolleybuses. While the one on the left is unidentifiable, the one on the right is the by now roofless 41 (OC 1141). 41 had been available for the opening of the Coventry Road 94 route on 7 January 1934 and by the time of its withdrawal had achieved 385,156 miles in service. To the right is an all-over blue-painted 291 (EOG 291), a Metro-Cammell-bodied Leyland Titan TD6c, that had arrived in Bird's yard on 17 June 1952 and was subsequently scrapped. (D. R. Harvey Collection)

53 (OC 1153)
Standing on their wheels in the clay at the bottom of the quarry used by Bird's in the summer of 1952 are Metro-Cammell-bodied Leyland TTBD2 trolleybuses 53 (OC 1153) and 63 (OC 1163). These GEC 80 hp trolleybuses had been the mainstay of the fleet from 1934 until the original 92 and 93 routes were extended from Yardley as the 94 and 95 routes respectively on 5 July 1936. Wandering around the site it had a most evocative smell, which seemed to be a mixture of old engine oil and rabbit droppings! (R. Marshall)

57 (OC 1157)
Five months after the abandonment of the trolleybuses in Birmingham, the trolleybus fleet were parked with their tyres still inflated as if all that was required to make them run again was a set of overhead wires! MCCW-bodied Leyland TTBD2 six-wheeler 57 (OC 1157) stands next to unidentified members of the same 17–66 class at the front of three rows of trolleybuses, with no evidence that any start to their scrapping has begun. (J. C. Brown)

58 (OC 1158)

Above: By the summer of 1952 the scene at Bird's had changed dramatically. With their trolleybooms blowing in the wind, the trolleybuses had been stripped of their tyres and glass as a concerted start was made to remove their aluminium roof panels and reduce them to their skeletal frames. On the left is 58 (OC 1158), while in front of the anonymous 79–90 class Leyland TB7, identifiable by its nearside trafficator fitment, is 69 (COX 69), one of the 1937 MCCW-bodied Leyland TB5s. (K. Moody)

65 (OC 1165)

Below: Coventry Road depot was also known as Arthur Street, after the side street that ran along the western side of the premises. The street's grim nineteenth-century three-storey terraces stand in a state of terminal decay as another of Bird's AEC Matadors turns into the street towing six-wheel Leyland TTBD2 trolleybus 65 (OC 1165) to the scrapyard. This trolleybus was one of four that were not in service on the opening day of the Coventry Road depot on 7 January 1934, being just two days too late. This rigid tow was undertaken by Bird's, who were responsible for clearing the whole fleet of seventy-four trolleybuses between the afternoon of Saturday 30 June 1951 and the evening of Sunday 1 July. The trip to Stratford was a colossal task, as each lorry had to undertake a round trip of nearly 50 miles. At least six lorries were used and with a top towing speed of only about 20 mph, there was an almost continuous shuttle between Coventry Road depot and the scrapyard throughout that weekend. The reason Bird's used Arthur Street was that it served as a shortcut to Stratford Road in Sparkbrook, before embarking on the 23-mile journey to Bird's yard. (L. W. Perkins)

68 (COX 68)

Above: The Coventry Road fleet remained intact until February and March 1951, when Leyland six-wheelers 24, 31, 51 and 52 were taken out of service and stored. In the last weeks of operation a number of others were removed from service. Parked next to the entrance of the depot, they were towed away for scrap on the final day of operation by the scrap merchant W. T. Bird to the Stratford-upon-Avon graveyard of withdrawn buses. These three dusty vehicles had obviously been taken out of service some days before. Four-wheeled Leyland TB5 68 (COX 68) and Leyland TTBD2 17 (OC 1117), in company with another of the six-wheelers, have had their destination blinds removed and their fleet numbers, civic crests and legal ownership painted out. This was normal BCT practice when a vehicle was withdrawn, but it did not really conceal the identity of the individual vehicles. (L. W. Perkins)

69 (COX 69)

Below: 69 (COX 69), a MCCW H29/24R-bodied Leyland TB5 that had entered service on 9 September 1937, is pulled out from Coventry Road depot behind one of Bird's ex-RAF 4x4 AEC Matador 0853s for the 23-mile tow to Stratford. Over 9,000 of these lorries were built and at the end of the Second World War a large number were snapped up for heavy haulage duties; Bird's found these fairly new four-wheel drive vehicles to be extremely useful towing vehicles. Amazingly, as this mass exodus from the depot was taking place, the normal Saturday trolleybus service continued as though it was just another day. (L. W. Perkins)

73 (COX 73)

Above: Not all of the seventy-four Coventry Road trolleybuses were collected from the depot on 30 June 1951. Eight six-wheelers, one of the COX-registered trolleybuses and three of the final FOK batch went to Cunliffe of Handsworth Wood for storage until there was space at Bird's Stratford yard. The solitary COX vehicle was 73, which had been the last official 94 service trolleybus and in the course of its fourteen years in service had clocked up 336,129 miles. It stands forlornly in Cunliffe's Wellington Road yard and had to wait until the following year before it was collected by Bird's. (D. R. Harvey Collection)

75 (COX 75)

Below: Around thirty of the Birmingham trolleybus fleet stand in Bird's scrapyard in Stratford a few days after the trolleybuses had run their last journeys along Coventry Road in Birmingham. On the left is 75 (COX 75), a Leyland TB5 with a MCCW H29/24R body that entered service on 22 September 1937, and the six-wheeled 23 (OC 1123), a Leyland TTBD2 also with a MCCW body but with a H33/25R layout, and which dated from the opening day of the Coventry Road trolleybus service on 7 January 1934. It looks as though Mr Bird has only to erect some overhead and he could run a service around Stratford with these trolleybuses. Despite being devoid of destination blinds, fleet numbers, legal lettering and municipal crests, the trolleybuses look in remarkably good condition for vehicles about to be broken up. (Stratford Guild Library)

82 (FOK 82)

Above: On Saturday 30 June 1951 the last trolleybuses were prepared for service as per normal. This was the last day of trolleybus operation on the 94 service along Coventry Road, as the last Lode Lane services had run the previous evening. Leyland TB7 82 (FOK 82), to the left of the pillar, which had first entered service on 16 February 1940, waits to go into service for the last time. These last MCCW trolleybuses had a slightly increased seating capacity of one, making them a H30/24R layout. They could be distinguished from the COX batch by their lack of guttering over the front top-deck windows, a style found on all motorbuses registered in the EOG and FOF series. On the right is the first of the Leyland six-wheelers, 17 (OC 1117); along with several other trolleybuses, it had already been taken out of service and has had its fleet number painted out and its destination blinds removed. In the background stand the new replacement Daimler CVD6s with Metro-Cammell bodies. (D. R. Harvey Collection)

83 (FOK 83)

Overleaf above: Bird's of Stratford had attempted to sell the FOK-registered trolleybuses to South Africa, but the deal fell through and only the bodies of Nos 83 and 90 were used again. Both trolleybuses were mounted on new Bristol K6G chassis by Silcox of Pembroke Dock. 83, a 1940 Leyland TB7 with a MCCW H30/24R body, had entered service in February 1940 as part of the new fleet intended to replace the 1932 half-cab Leyland TB2s on the Nechells route. The Nechells service was prematurely closed due to its infringement of the blackout regulations when travelling to and from Washwood Heath Garage as a skate had to be employed. By now registered ODE 402, former trolleybus 83 would remain in service until 1967, when it was usually on hire to Tarmac to transport their civil engineering workers. (A. J. Douglas)

90 (FOK 90)

Overleaf below: Leyland TB7 90 (FOK 90) was numerically the last of the twelve Metro-Cammell H30/24R trolleybuses and entered service on 20 February 1940. It was used on the two final tours of the Birmingham system on Sunday 17 June and Sunday, 24 June 1951 and closed the system after carrying Mr W. H. Smith, the general manager, as well as members of the Transport Department back to Coventry Road depot at about 12.05 a.m. on 1 July 1951, by which time it had run 259,493 miles in service. So 90 really was Birmingham's last trolleybus in every sense! The MCCW body of 90 was mounted on a new Bristol K6G chassis, which had been bought by Silcox as one of a batch immediately before Bristol Commercial Vehicles stopped accepting new chassis orders after their nationalisation in 1948. The chassis were gradually put into service after a period of storage and the former FOK 90's body was put on the Bristol chassis and registered ODE 401. The front dash was cut to allow the fitting of the Bristol radiator, leaving the rest of the body still recognisable as a Birmingham trolleybus. It is dumped opposite Silcox's garage in Pembroke Dock after it had been finally withdrawn in September 1961. (D. Akrigg)

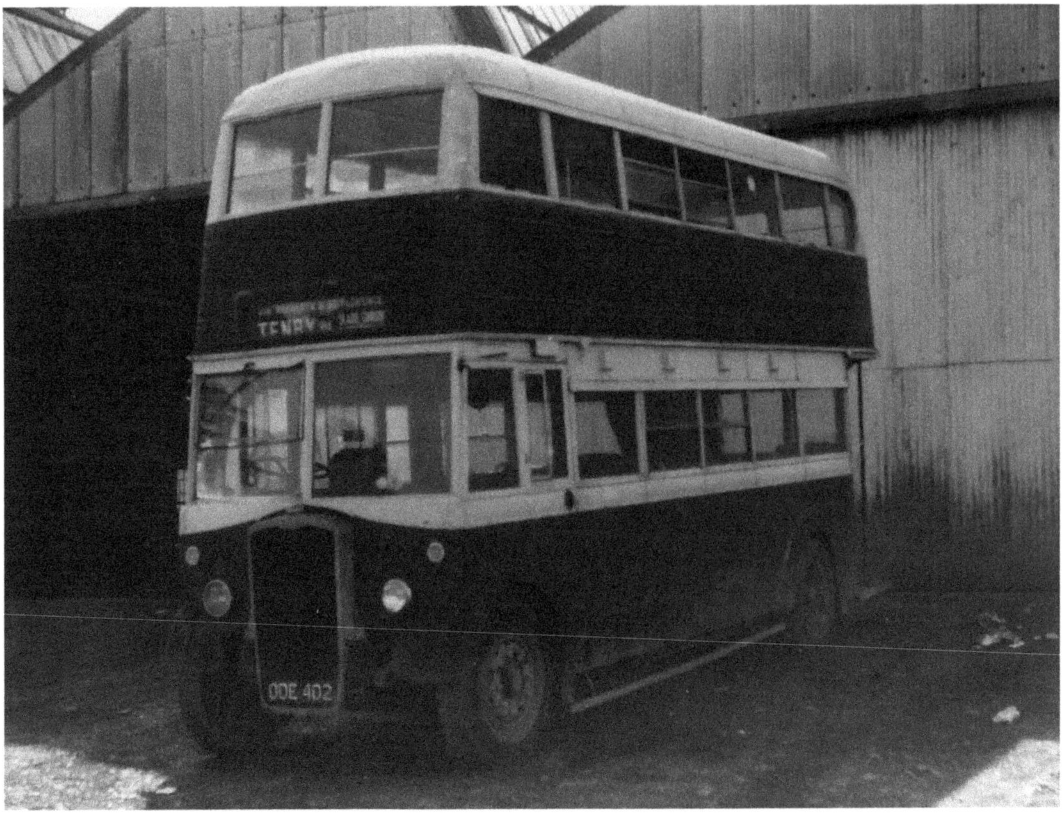
ODE 402

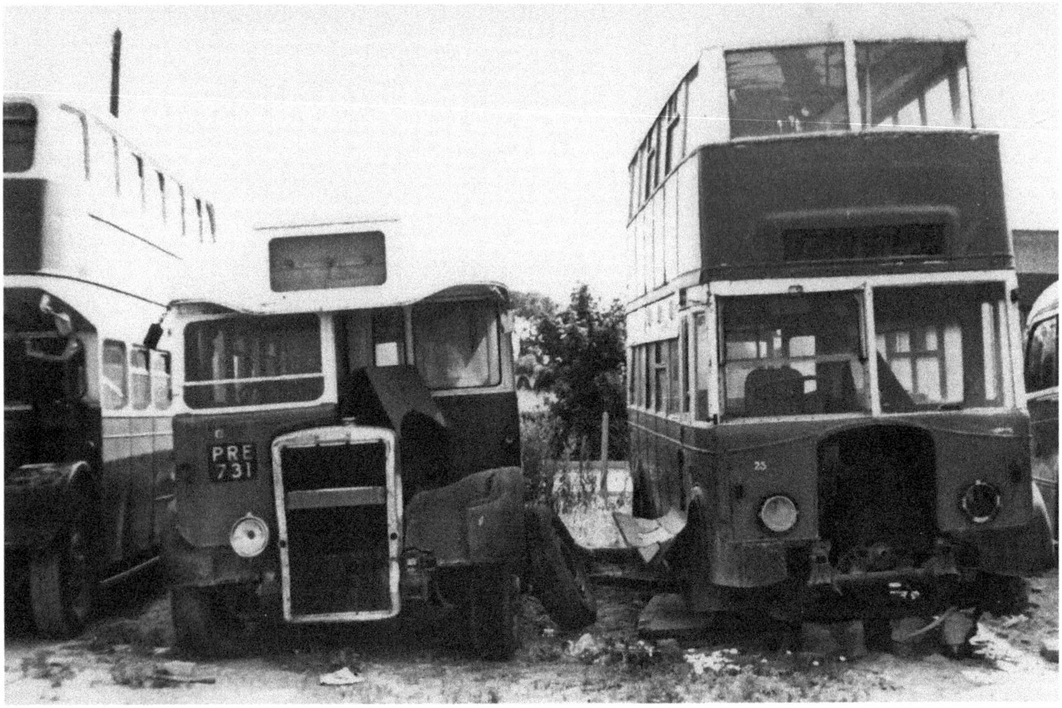
PRE 731

7
Post-War Buses, 1947–1948

1491 (GOE 491)
The first batch of post-war buses to be withdrawn was taken out of service on 31 December 1961 and most were sold to T. J. Richardson of Dudley Road East, in Brades Village near Oldbury. 1491 (GOE 491), a Daimler CVA6 with a MCCW H30/24R body, first entered service on 12 July 1947 and was sold to Richardson's after its withdrawal on 31 January 1961. These bodies had unique thin-section body pillars and square-cornered inset windows of a type never ordered again by BCT. After two years 1491 was subsequently sold to Smith, the Bilston-based scrap dealer. On the right are two Daimler CVG6s with Metro-Cammell bodywork, 1569 (GOE 569) and 1573 (GOE 573), both of which were scrapped during 1962. The interloper is RN 8186, the former Ribble MS 1802, a Leyland Titan TD5 dating from 1938 and rebodied by ECW in 1948. (L. Mason)

1495 (GOE 495)
Above: Looking a bit dusty, but quite serviceable, is 1495 (GOE 495), which had entered service on 18 July 1947 from Harborne Garage. The Daimler CVA6s had a flexible-mounted AEC 7.57-litre engine, which, coupled to the fairly lightweight 7 tons 12 cwt of the Metro-Cammell H30/24R body, gave the seventy-five buses in the class a very comfortable and pleasant-sounding ride. Unfortunately, the first-in-first-out principal made these buses prime candidates for early withdrawal, as in this case on New Year's Eve 1961, having totalled almost 387,000 miles in service. It is parked in Richardson's yard in company with 1630 (GOE 630), a Daimler CVG6 that was eventually sold to Andies Coaches of Nechells, and a Smethwick-registered 1945-vintage Maudslay Maharajah six-wheeled flatbed lorry. (A. D. Broughall)

1519 (GOE 519)
Below: Standing in the snow-covered yard of Smith, a dealer based in Bilston, with Wolverhampton Corporation Park Royal-bodied Guy BT trolleybus 653 (FJW 653) in front of them are six former Birmingham Daimler CVA6s. The nearest bus is 1519 (GOE 519) while only the next two, 1490 (GOE 490) and 1491 (GOE 491), are identifiable. All were sold to Richardson in Oldbury in late April 1962, having been withdrawn from service during 1961. This line-up of the BCT buses rather confirms that Richardson acted as a dealer and if they couldn't be sold for further use they disposed of them to smaller Black Country scrapyards. (A. D. Broughall)

1530 (GOE 530)

Above: The first post-war Birmingham City Transport bus to be taken out of service was 1530 (GOE 530), a Daimler CVA6 with a Metro-Cammell H30/24R body. It had entered service on 1 October 1947, but when working on the Outer Circle 11 route on 7 January 1961 had skidded going down Marsh Hill in the snow and overturned onto its nearside. This caused quite a lot of frame damage, which is visible as it stands already partially stripped alongside the still complete 1115 (CVP 215), a 1937 Daimler COG5 that was withdrawn in December 1960. (D. R. Harvey Collection)

1536 (GOE 536)

Below: Minus its headlights, 1536 (GOE 536), a Daimler CVA6, was new on 1 October 1947, and although having been given a new five-year CoF ticket, it was prematurely withdrawn on 30 November 1961 after an engine fire, which caused severe damage to the Metro-Cammell engine bay and bodywork. As a result it arrived under tow to Richardson's as a non-runner, but was actually sold on to a scrap merchant in Bilston. (A. D. Broughall)

1573 (GOE 573)

Richardson's yard was in Dudley Road East, just visible on the left, while in the foreground the site's western boundary was the Gower branch of the Birmingham Canal that linked James Brindley's Old Birmingham Level 'crooked ditch' of 1771 with the straight Wolverhampton Level with a summit at 453 feet built to the design of Thomas Telford in 1828. At least sixteen of the forty-nine BCT buses purchased by Richardson's at auction on 27 April 1962 are visible here. This purchase consisted of thirty-two Daimler CVA6s, some thirteen Daimler CVG6s, three Daimler CVD6s and 1748 (HOV 748), a Brush-bodied Leyland Titan PD2/1 that went under a low bridge at Scriber's Lane, Hall Green in August 1961. Identifiable are the rears of 1573 (GOE 573), a Daimler CVG6, Daimler CVA6 1485 (GOE 485) and, towards the right, 1796 (HOV 796), which was taken out of service on 28 February 1962. (L. Mason)

1580 (GOE 580)

Dumped in the waste ground alongside Washwood Heath Garage is Daimler CVG6 1580 (GOE 580). This bus was withdrawn on 31 May 1963 and, along with 1585, was transferred to the City Lighting Department, based in Cambridge Street. Whatever their intended use was going to be, neither bus was ever used, and so 1580, by now cannibalised for its Gardner 6LW 8.4-litre engine, waits for the arrival of the scrap man – in this case Smith of Stopsley near Luton, who would collect both 1580 and 1585 during October 1965. (R. Manison)

Post-War Buses, 1947–1948

1596 (GOE 596)
Two of the Metro-Cammell-bodied Daimler CVG6s built in 1947 are being driven north in September 1967 en route to be scrapped by Wombwell Diesels. Leading the way towards their own execution is 1596 (GOE 596), which had entered service on 1 January 1948 and is being followed by 1563 (GOE 563), which was two months older. 1563 had been retired on 31 July 1966 while 1596 was taken out of service on 31 October 1966. Both buses are being driven by employees of Wombwell Diesels. (J. S. Cockshott)

1602 (GOE 602)
Most of the buses that went to Richardson's were vehicles whose CoFs had expired and they became surplus to requirements. With a repaint and an overhaul they were still quite serviceable buses, but with the economic need to reduce the fleet size and modernise the stock, they were withdrawn. 1602 (GOE 602) was an accident victim and was withdrawn on 31 August 1961; it arrived at Brades Village after being sold to Richardson at the beginning of May the following year. It not only suffered severe damage to the driver's cab but the chassis had been terminally twisted in the accident. (L. Mason)

1641 (GOE 641)
Above: 1641 (GOE 641) was withdrawn from Acocks Green Garage on 29 February 1964 but languished inside the premises for a number of months. The following summer an Omnibus Society Tour included a visit to Acocks Green and the dusty 1641 was started up and driven to the small back yard next to the North Warwickshire railway line, where it was duly photographed. Fifteen of these AEC Regent III 0961 RT-types were delivered to Birmingham with standard Park Royal H29/25R four-bay bodywork, equipped with Birmingham-style fixtures and fittings, and an enormously long sloping windscreen designed to eliminate interior light reflections at night, but which was out of proportion with the rest of the front due to the low mounted radiator. It was sold to Hoyle's in August 1964 and driven to Yorkshire 'under its own steam' for breaking up. (D. F. Parker)

1646 (GOE 646)
Below: Derelict in Washwood Heath yard on 27 June 1965 is the first of the pre-production batch of ten Crossley-bodied Crossley DD42/6s. 1646 (GOE 646) entered service on 25 May 1949 from Liverpool Street Garage, where it was put to work on the 15 and 16 services. It was withdrawn along with all but two of the ten Crossleys on 30 June 1964, and what panels the garage body makers haven't stripped off, the local children have made up for by getting into the unattended yard and breaking most of the windows on the bus. 1646 would shortly be sold to Smith, the Luton scrap merchant. (R. Manison)

296 (HOJ 396)

Above: Perhaps one of the most important post-war buses to be built, 296 (HOJ 396) is parked as a withdrawn vehicle in Washwood Heath Garage yard in the spring of 1968, having been withdrawn on 31 October 1967. BCT had previously been a valued customer of Leyland Motors in 1938, ordering all the 135-built specially designed Titan TD6c chassis to its own specification. The thinking was that for their post-war orders Birmingham would again use Leyland as its alternative supplier, especially as it had the new large 9.8-litre-engined PD2 that was seen as an ideal model for Birmingham. This was the second prototype Leyland Titan PD2, the first being chassis EX1-registered CVA 430. EX2, completed at the end of June 1947, was given the chassis number 470848. It had a Leyland PD1-style body but modified to have the lower cab apron finishing halfway down the offside mudguard. The Leyland body had a seating configuration of H30/26R. The bus was registered HOJ 396 and given the next fleet number after the 1939 batch of Leyland Titan TD6cs. The bus was delivered to BCT in the third week of September and entered service on the 29th of that month. 296 was allocated to Yardley Wood Garage for all its life, where it was a regular performer on the 24 service to Warstock. At first glance it looked like a member of Hockley Garage's 2131 class. Its registration number plate was carried below the windscreen and the arrangement of its half-drop opening saloon windows was also different. It had to be manned by tall conductors as the platform bell was very difficult to reach. 296 was the first post-war vehicle to operate for twenty years, although it only achieved 312,000 miles in service. It is parked alongside 1657 (HOV 657) and both were sold to Hartwood Finance in June 1968. (D. R. Harvey Collection)

1660 (HOV 660)

Overleaf above: Lined up in Washwood Heath Garage yard are three withdrawn Leyland Titan PD2 Sp with Brush H30/24R bodywork. 1660, 1682 and 1664, with matching HOV registrations dating from September and October 1948, were all marked up with the letter 'C' to show that they were ready for collection by Wombwell Diesels in August 1968. They had been stored in Yardley Wood Garage since, in the case of 1660, February 1968, with the other two having been withdrawn on 31 March 1968. (A. Yates)

1747 (HOV 747)

Below: The engineless 1747 (HOV 747) is parked at the back of Washwood Heath Garage yard, having had the Leyland 0.600 9.8-litre engine retrieved and placed in store for possible further use. One of the 100 Brush-bodied Leyland Titan PD2 Sp, 1747 entered service on 3 Mach 1949. It spent its entire life working from Perry Barr Garage, operating on their long 11 Outer Circle service and the cross-city 29A route from Aldridge to the Solihull boundary in Hall Green. It was withdrawn on 31 October 1967 and was sold to Wombwell Diesels for scrap in February 1968. (D. R. Harvey Collection)

1748 (HOV 748)

Above: The only Leyland purchased for scrapping by Richardson of Oldbury was 1748 (HOV 748) on 27 April 1962. This Brush-bodied Leyland Titan PD2 Sp had been partially de-roofed when it tried to get underneath Scribers Lane in August 1961, when the driver attempted to take a shortcut to Yardley Wood Garage while returning from the Hall Green terminus of the 29A route. On the left is 1521 (GOE 521), a 1947 MCCW-bodied Daimler CVA6 that was broken up, while on the right is 1556 (GOE 556), a Daimler CVG6 that was sold for further service to Johnson of Birmingham. (A. D. Broughall)

1764 (HOV 764)

Below: In the mid-1960s, the forecourt of Bird's Commercial Vehicles alongside Birmingham Road in Stratford-upon-Avon was used to park recently arrived buses driven from Birmingham. Within days the buses were driven across the forecourt before turning left and passing the night-watchman's caravan before going down the steep slope and into the quarry to wait for the scrap man's torch to commence dismantling. 1764 (HOV 764), 1815 (HOV 815) and 1797 (HOV 797) had all been taken out of service between July and September 1963 and were three of the thirty-three MCCW-bodied Daimler CVD6s sold to Bird's in February 1964. It was a shame that these well-maintained buses were withdrawn so early. (A. D. Broughall)

1776 (HOV 776)
Above: Six of the 1948-vintage Daimler CVD6s have recently arrived at Bird's quarry and all appear to be complete. After a few more months most of these buses would be well on the way to being broken up. All these buses, including 1776, 1795, 1818, 1789, 1772 and 1812, with matching HOV registrations, were sold at auction in February 1964, having been taken out of service in the summer of 1963. (L. Mason)

1781 (HOV 781)
Below: After spending most of its working life operating from Coventry Road Garage, 1781 (HOV 781), withdrawn on 31 July 1963, was parked up in the yard at the back of the garage that led off the distant Arthur Street. 1781 entered service on 1 May 1948, initially operating from Liverpool Street Garage until transferred to Coventry Road. After the Stechford tram routes' 301 class four-wheeled trams were moved out on 2 October 1948 there was enough space to take these new Daimler CVD6s, which would be used on the replacement 53 and 54 bus routes. 1781 would shortly be taken to Bird's in Stratford in the spring of 1964. (D. R. Harvey)

1803 (HOV 803)

Above: 1803 (HOV 803), a Daimler CVD6 with a Metro-Cammell H30/24R body, entered service on 1 July 1948 as just another standard member of the 1756–1843 class. However, within a few months of entering service the bus was taken into Tyburn Road Works and fitted with a set of triple indicator destination boxes that would become the standard equipment on the 'New Look' Crossleys, Daimlers and Guys. It spent a lot of its career operating from Hockley Garage and was withdrawn on 31 August 1963. It is seen here standing in Bird's scrapyard soon after its arrival. (A. D. Broughall)

1810 (HOV 810)

Overleaf above: The ultimate indignity for a bus sold to Bird's for scrapping was that, once stripped of any useful parts, a bus would be tipped onto its side to extract any further inaccessible chassis parts. Any bus thus tipped over tended to be abandoned for many years before it was finally dismantled. 1810 (HOV 810), propped up with the remains of an earlier broken-up vehicle, has revealed most of the chassis components of the Daimler CVD6. 1810 had arrived at Bird's in the spring of 1964, along with other distant buses from the same class. (A. D. Broughall)

1818 (HOV 818)

Overleaf below: Recently arrived at Quinton Garage sometime in October 1963 is 1818 (HOV 818), a 1948 Daimler CVD6 with a MCCW H30/24R body. It is yet another of the batch that, despite its apparently good condition, was to be sold to Bird's in February 1964 and broken up. The main reason why these buses went so early was that the Daimler CD6 engine, despite being a very quiet and refined-sounding unit, burnt a lot of engine oil and was somewhat awkward and time-consuming to service. These Daimler CVD6s were not usually stored at Quinton Garage as they were mainly dumped at Washwood Heath or Lea Hall Garages. (A. D. Broughall)

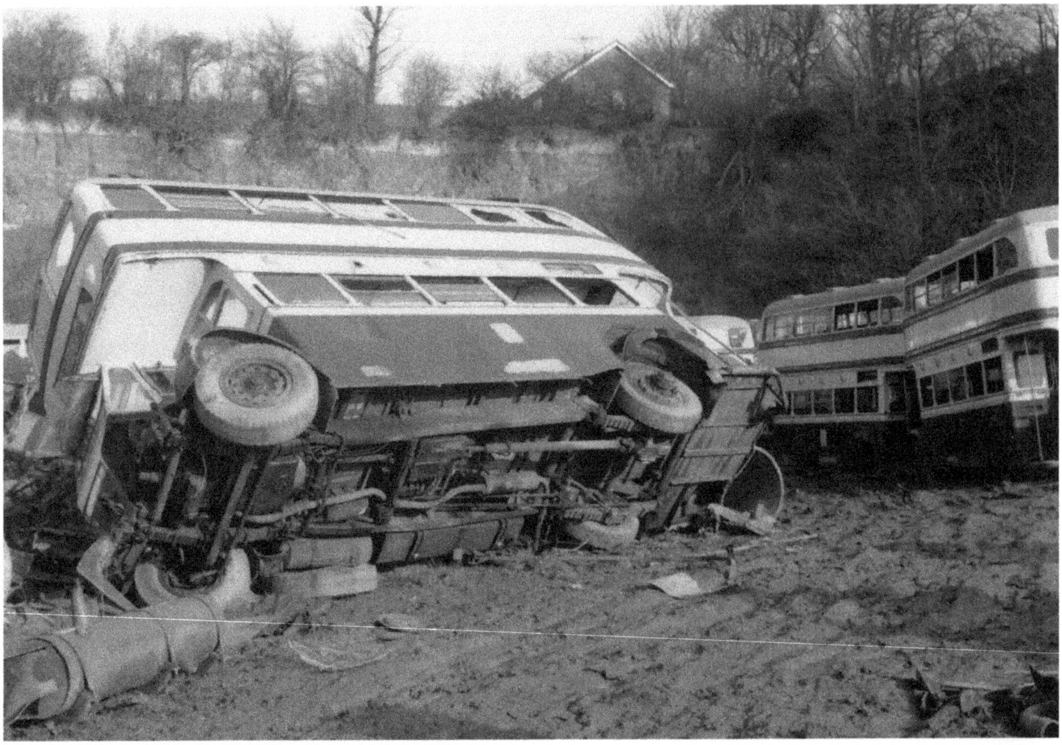

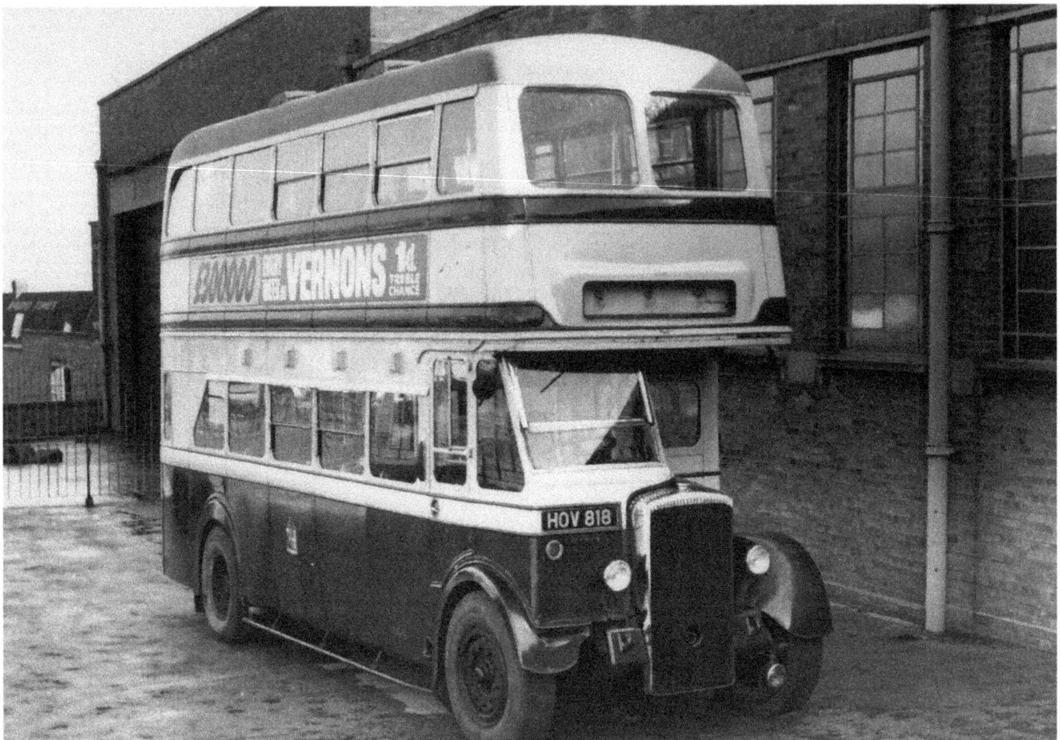
VERNONS
HOV 818

1834 (HOV 834)

Above: Recalling the breaking up of the earlier Birmingham trolleybuses and the pre-war Daimler COG5s, the shell of 1834 (HOV 834) stands in the bottom of Bird's scrapyard stripped of its roof and side body panels. As with many of the CVD6s, there was no second-hand value for the 8.6-litre Daimler CD6 engine and so they were left in the chassis. 1834 had been purchased at auction by Bird in February 1964, having originally been delicensed on 31 July 1963. (D. R. Harvey Collection)

1841 (HOV 841)

Below: An unusual second-hand sale was of 1841 (HOV 841) and 1843 (HOV 843). These two Daimler CVD6s with MCCW H30/24R bodywork were both sold in August 1964 to Oldham Corporation. This Lancashire municipality had a large number of buses compulsorily taken off the road by the local Traffic Commissioners due to poor maintenance, including a number of Crossley-bodied Daimler CVD6s. Many northern operators either hired or sold elderly buses to Oldham for further use, but while Birmingham sold Oldham two Daimler CVD6s, despite their good condition, BCT made the proviso that they could not be operated and could only be used for spares! Thus 1841 and 1843, behind it, are parked engineless in Oldham Corporation's bus garage. (P. Cain)

8

Post-War Buses, 1949–1950

1860 (HOV 860)
The eighty-seven 'HOV-Gardners' that entered service between November 1948 and October 1949 were regarded as the real workhorses of the early BCT post-war bus fleet. They were allocated mainly to Highgate Road, Lea Hall and Liverpool Street, where they could be found operating on the Inner Circle 8 route, the City Circle 19 service, the long 28 route to Great Barr, north-west of the City Centre but by way of the eastern and northern suburbs in Birmingham, and also on the long 16 route from Hamstead across the city to Garrett's Green. These were unglamorous routes but were generally busy and profitable. These Daimler CVG6s slogged their way on these heavily patronised routes for up to nineteen years. 1860 (HOV 860) is parked in Washwood Heath Garage yard waiting to be taken to Wombwell Diesels in the autumn of 1968. (A. Yates)

Post-War Buses, 1949–1950   83

1879 (HOV 879)
Above: Lined up in echelon against the Ridgacre Road wall in Quinton Garage yard are 1879 (HOV 879) and 1586 (GOE 586), as well as 1871, 1893 and 1898, with matching HOV registrations. All of these Metro-Cammell-bodied Daimler CVG6s were taken out of service in November 1963 and converted to snowploughs, replacing pre-war Daimler COG5s. What was strange was that both 1871 and 1879 were fully overhauled in 1962 and became some of the first buses to receive the small black waistrail fleet numbers. Every garage in Birmingham had at least one snowplough and most of them hardly turned a wheel until they were all withdrawn en mass in July 1971, having been taken over by WMPTE on 1 October 1969. Two months after they were taken out of use the thirty-three post-war snowploughs were sold to Wombwell Diesels. (E. V. Trigg)

1902 (HOV 902)
Below: With all its legal lettering, municipal crests and fleet numbers removed, 1902 (HOV 902), a Daimler CVG6 dating from 1 May 1949, has had to have a front end suspended tow to Wombwell Diesels in August 1967. The towing vehicle is the cut-down NKT 913, a 1951 Leyland Titan PD2/3 formerly numbered DH417 in the Maidstone & District fleet. Parked behind is an earlier Daimler CVG6 with a MCCW body 1626 (GOE 626), which entered service on 1 February 1948 and has been driven on the long journey to Barnsley. BCT buses were sold by auction and after acquisition by the scrap dealer a letter, in this case 'C', was chalked onto the lower-saloon front window in order for the dealer to recognise the buses he had bought. (A. J. Douglas)

1929 (HOV 929)

Above: Dumped at the rear of the waste ground next to Washwood Heath Garage are four withdrawn buses, each having incurred rear-end accident damage. On the left is 1929 (HOV 929), the penultimate exposed radiator Daimler CVG6 bought by BCT with the sort of Metro-Cammell body that was also supplied to Edinburgh and Newcastle Corporations. 1929 entered service on 2 October 1949 and was officially withdrawn on 31 December 1964, although its accident occurred sometime earlier. The leading bus against the garage wall is 2281 (JOJ 281), part of whose accident damage is a huge crease all the way up the offside rear of the body. Behind it is 2276 (JOJ 276), whose back platform had been caved in, while in the middle is 2269 (JOJ 269), which had been hit in the rear and severe damage was caused to the platform and the staircase. These last three buses were Crossley-bodied Crossley DD42/6s and dated from November and December 1949. All four buses were sold to Hoyle's of Barnsley for scrap in August 1964. (L. Mason)

1935 (HOV 935)

Below: Seven of the twelve Metro-Cammell-bodied Daimler CVD6s stand withdrawn alongside the former trolleybus perimeter road inside Park Lane Garage's site. Identifiable are 1935 (HOV 935), 1952 (HOV 952), 2000 (JOC 200) and 2007 (JOJ 7). These buses were loaned to Wolverhampton Corporation because of the premature conversion of the Fighting Cocks–Bilston–Willenhall 25 trolleybus route to motor bus operation, as a result of railway bridge rebuilding at Willenhall. These vehicles retained their Birmingham fleet numbers during their period on loan from 26 October 1964 and all were subsequently acquired by Wolverhampton Corporation in March 1965. All were withdrawn in February 1967 and all but one were sold to Gammell, a dealer based in Dudley Fields, Walsall. (D. R. Harvey Collection)

1996 (HOV 996)

Recently arrived at Taylor's scrapyard in Stafford in March 1965 is 1996 (HOV 996). 1996 was one of twenty-four of the class to be scrapped by Taylor's. This Daimler CVD6 had a Metro Cammell H30/24R body and entered service on 1 November 1949, operating from Coventry Road Garage. It was taken out of service on 31 August 1964. (2489 Group Collection)

2021 (JOJ 21)

The Washwood Heath site was used for the storage of buses waiting to be collected by the various dealers who had bought them from BCT by auction. 2021 (JOJ 21), a Daimler CVD6, entered service on 6 December 1949 and spent most of its operational life at Perry Barr Garage. Although withdrawn on New Year's Eve 1964, it spent nearly thirty months in store before being sold to the Hudley Trading Company of Wolverhampton. The engineless Crossley is 2346 (JOJ 346), the first of the class to have sliding saloon ventilators, which would be sold to Bird's for scrapping in May 1967. (A. Yates)

2067 (JOJ 67)
Above: Three of the 'New Look' concealed radiator Daimler CVD6s, 2067 (JOJ 67), 2050 (JOJ 50) and 2047 (JOJ 47), were bought by Wombwell Diesels but were scrapped at Banbury in February 1966. Four of these Daimler CVD6 buses were broken up in Banbury and, as per usual, the central part of the front cowling had been removed. After having their delivery delayed for nearly two years, the 100 buses in the 2031–2130 class of Daimler CVD6s enter service between September 1950 and August 1951 and all were withdrawn by the end of October 1966. (D. R. Harvey Collection)

2082 (JOJ 82)
Below: Although still complete, 2082 (JOJ 82), a concealed radiator Daimler CVD6, is gradually sinking into the cloying clay at the old brickworks quarry at Bird's scrapyard in Stratford on Saturday, 26 February 1966. The bus had only been acquired by Bird's during the previous month. These buses had been replaced by rear-engined BON-C-registered Daimler Fleetline CRG6LX and were sold with almost indecent haste for breaking up. (A. D. Packer)

2084 (JOJ 84)
Above: Waiting for scrapping to begin, Daimler CVD6s 2084 (JOJ 84) and 2108 (JOJ 108) have recently arrived at Wombwell Diesels in April 1967. 2084 was new on 1 March 1951 while 2108 arrived on 1 June 151 and both were withdrawn on 30 September 1966. Most New Look front buses suffered with hot or fading front brakes and most Crossleys, Daimler CVD6s and CVG6s, and Guy Arab III Sp and IV Sp had their full-length front wings cut back, which has been done on 2084, but, surprisingly, not on 2108. (T. W. W. Knowles)

2129 (JOJ 129)
Below: At least four Metro Cammell-bodied Daimler CVD6s to be parked up in Washwood Heath Garage yard in front of a number of exposed radiator Crossley DD42/6s include the recently arrived 2129 (JOJ 129) and 2076 (JOJ 76). Both had spent months in store since their withdrawal and they were sold to Hudley Trading of Wolverhampton in June 1967. The Crossleys in the distance include 2411 (JOJ 411) and 2267 (JOJ 267), which were sold to Wombwell Diesels for scrapping in March 1967. (L. Mason)

2141 (JOJ 141)

Lea Hall Garage yard was full of withdrawn buses in early 1968, including a large number of vehicle types that were never actually operated by the garage. All three body types fitted to BCT's Leyland Titan PD2/1s are represented, as well as an unidentified exposed radiator Crossley DD42/6. 2141 (JOJ 141) was one of fifty standard Leyland-bodied Leyland Titan PD2/1s bought virtually 'off the peg'. Unlike their pre-war equivalents they had the normal Leyland L-shaped staircase and were fitted with standard thin-backed Leyland seating, which in the lower saloon had a Leyland-patterned moquette rather than the normal BCT style. It had entered service on 25 March 1949 and spent its entire career operating from Hockley Garage until the end of November 1967. It was sold to Hartwood Finance in June 1968, as was withdrawn 2184 (JOJ 184), the Park Royal-bodied Leyland Titan PD2/1 that had been fitted with an early version of the semi-automatic pneumocyclic gearbox in February 1958. As a result of this experimental gearbox, 2184 sounded like a Leyland Atlantean PDR1/1. On the extreme left is Brush-bodied 1732 (HOV 732), which would be moved to Wombwell Diesels after being sold to them for scrap in March 1968. (V. France)

2156 (JOJ 156)

Parked in Washwood Heath Garage yard in the spring of 1968 are 2156 (JOJ 156) and 2157 (JOJ 157). Both of these Leyland-bodied Leyland Titan PD2/1s are waiting collection by Wombwell Diesels in August 1968, whose identifying letter 'C' is chalked on the lower-saloon front window. In view of their condition it is a fair bet to assume they were driven to Yorkshire under their own power. Both buses entered service on 1 May 1949 and were withdrawn on 31 January 1968. (G. Yates)

2166 (JOJ 166)
Above: The last four of the class, 2131, 2140, 2142 and 2146, somehow contrived to outlast all the rest of the Leyland-bodied Leylands by some six months. In February 1968 at least ten earlier withdrawals of the same time are awaiting disposal in Lea Hall Garage yard, having only recently arrived for storage. Only 2166, 2168, 2167 and 2174, with matching JOJ registrations, are identifiable and all were taken out of service on 29 February 1968, three being collected by Wombwell Diesels five months later. (R. F. deBöer)

2185 (JOJ 185)
Below: A few parts including some of the glass windows have already been removed from 2185 (JOJ 185) as it stands in Wombwell Diesel's yard in April 1970 alongside a Bournemouth Weymann-bodied Sunbeam MF2 trolleybus. This Leyland Titan PD2/1 had a Park Royal H29/25R body and entered service on 8 October 1949, operating from Hockley Garage. These fifty buses completed the order for 200 Leyland double-deckers. At 7 feet 6 inches wide, they were the only PD2/1s built with this style of Park Royal body, which was similar to the fifteen on the AEC Regent III RTs of 1947, but were of five rather than four-bay construction. The buses conformed to most of Birmingham's stringent interior requirements, but had a Park Royal-style L-shaped staircase. Although a non-standard body design, the resultant vehicle was an extremely handsome bus. 2185 was taken out of service on 31 December 1968 and was sold to Wombwell Diesels in September 1969. (R. F. deBöer)

2191 (JOJ 191)

Above: Recently withdrawn 2191 (JOJ 191) and 2226 (JOJ 226) have been parked in Washwood Heath Garage yard in the autumn of 1969. They are two Leyland Titan PD2/1s with Park Royal H29/25R bodywork. 2191 entered service on 1 November 1949 from Hockley Garage and was one of the last of the class to be taken out of service, on 31 July 1969. It was then placed in store and eventually sold for scrap to Rollinson, Carlton, in January 1970. 2226 was new on 1 March 1950 and for nearly all of its working life was allocated to Rosebery Street Garage for use on the Dudley Road services. 2226 was initially withdrawn on 31 January 1969, before being put back into service on 1 May that year for two months, and then passed to WMPTE as a withdrawn bus. It was also sold to Rollinson, Carlton, in January 1970 for scrap. The first fifteen buses of the 2181–2230 class, including 2191 on the left, were delivered from Park Royal with the front destination box about 3 inches too high, and, as a result, the middle blue livery band above the cab was straight and did not dip beneath the route display. From bus 2196 the destination box was lowered while the blue livery band had a dip in it and a thinner centre section, which is found on 2226. (D. Skeffington)

2193 (JOJ 193)

Below: Standing in Hockley Garage yard on 27 August 1966 is 2193 (JOJ 193), which is having its charred bodywork damped down by firemen. This Leyland Titan PD2/1 had a Park Royal H29/25R body and was formerly withdrawn just four days later; after a short period dumped in Washwood Heath Garage yard it was sold to Wombwell Diesels in December 1966. The bus had been attacked by an arsonist setting fire to the upper saloon. It was only the third member of the 2181–2230 class to be withdrawn. (D. R. Harvey Collection)

2203 (JOJ 203)

Above: Driving along the Sandiacre bypass, Nottingham, is 2203 (JOJ 203), another Leyland Titan PD2/1 with a Park Royal H29/25R body, which entered service on 1 January 1950 and was withdrawn on 30 November 1968, having spent most of its life based at Rosebery Street Garage. It is being driven to Hartwood Finance in the summer of 1969 to be scrapped. Some of these were among the last exposed radiator buses to be operated by Birmingham City Transport. (T. W. W. Knowles)

2211 (JOJ 211)

Below: Both 2211 (JOJ 211) and 2229 (JOJ 229), the only one of the class to be operated by WMPTE, were sold to Wombwell Diesels in January 1970. This pair of Park Royal-bodied Leyland Titan PD2/1s were cut down to three-quarter-length open-topped towing wagons and operated on trade plates. Both towing former Hastings Tramways Sunbeam W4 trolleybuses with Weymann bodies, the cut-down 2211 and 2229 buses are leaving Birchills depot in Walsall in May 1970 on their way to Wombwell Diesels. (R. F. Mack)

2215 (JOJ 215)

Above: Lined up and engineless in Hartwood Finance's Barnsley scrapyard in the autumn of 1969 are three Leyland Titan PD2/1 with Park Royal H29/25R bodies. The nearest one is unidentifiable but the next two ready to be broken up are 2215 (JOJ 215) and 2221 (JOJ 221). The fourth BCT bus is a Leyland Titan PD2/1 with a Leyland H30/26R body and 2631 (JOJ 631), a MCCW H30//24R-bodied Daimler CVD6 that was one of the buses that replaced the Coventry Road trolleybuses in 1 July 1951. (D. R. Harvey Collection)

2227 (JOJ 227)

Below: After being involved in an accident in February 1965 it was decided to condemn 2227 (JOJ 227), a Leyland Titan PD2/1 with a Park Royal H29/25R body. The front wings could have been replaced, for at the time the bus was not intended to be withdrawn for about five years; however, the upper-saloon body pillar damage made it uneconomic to repair. 2227 is parked just inside Lea Hall Garage's top side gate in the spring of 1965. It was sold to Smith of Stopsley near Luton in October 1965 and was promptly broken up. (PM Photography)

2238 (JOJ 238)

Above: Two rather dusty Leyland Tiger PS2/1s with Weymann B34F bodies are 2238 (JOJ 238) of 1 August 1950 and 2247 (JOJ 247), which entered service just four days later on 4 August 1950. Both stand withdrawn in Yardley Wood Garage on 16 June 1971. Originally withdrawn on 31 May 1965, 2238 was reinstated fourteen months later before finally being taken out of service on 31 March 1969, while 2247 was withdrawn two months later and, being loaned twice to Potteries Motor Traction, was being returned on 11 May 1970. Both buses were sold to Cowley's, a dealer based in Blackpool, by August 1972. 2238 is being guarded by the garage's cat. (E. V. Trigg)

2248 (JOJ 248)

Below: Having been taken out of service in March 1966, 2248 (JOJ 248) was the first of the Weymann-bodied Leyland Tiger PS2/1s to be withdrawn. It had been involved in a severe accident, incurring extensive damage to the rear of the vehicle. It is waiting in Washwood Heath Garage yard in 1967 before being sold to Wombwell Diesels in August of that year. Alongside it on the right is 1598 (GOE 598), a 1948 Daimler CVG6 with a Metro-Cammell H30/24R body that was withdrawn on 31 October 1966. On the left stands 1730 (HOV 730), a Brush-bodied Leyland Titan PD2/1Sp of February 1949 that was taken out of service on 31 March 1967. All three of these buses were sold to Wombwell Diesels for scrapping in August 1967. (L. Mason)

2265 (JOJ 265)

Above: Birmingham's only underfloor-engined single-deckers to be built were five Leyland Olympic HR40s with Weymann B36F bodies. These buses entered service between July and August 1950 and replaced five of the Leyland Tiger PS2/1s. They were initially employed on the Elmdon Airport service before being used on the inter-urban 27 route. The five then opened the new 4 service to Pool Farm from Cotteridge on 1 December 1963, and the 26 route introduced on 11 September 1967 from Saltley to the new Bromford Bridge Estate. All were sold to the Carlton scrap dealer Pickersgill & Laverack in September 1969, just before WMPTE took over BCTs operations. 2265 (JOJ 265), the last of the quintet, is parked in Washwood Heath Garage yard on 27 August 1969 along with 636 (AOG 636), a 1934 Daimler COG5 converted to a lorry in 1947 and immediately withdrawn after being taken over in October 1969 by WMPTE. (D. R. Harvey Collection)

2278 (JOJ 278)

Below: Waiting for scrapping to begin, 2278 (JOJ 278), a Crossley-bodied Crossley DD42/6, had recently been bought at auction at Wombwell Diesels in April 1967. It was one of twenty-two of these exposed radiator Crossleys to enter service in December 1949 and was taken out of service in December 1966 after spending most of its life at Selly Oak Garage. Next to it is 1540 (GOE 540), a late 1947-vintage Daimler CVA6 with a MCCW body, which was one of a trio that survived in service until 31 July 1966, some four and a half years after the first of these buses were withdrawn. (T. W. W. Knowles)

2307 (JOJ 307)

Above: By the time the exposed radiator Crossley DD42/6s were being withdrawn, Bird's had moved from their Birmingham Road site to the large military site at Long Marston. At about the same time, the previously highly favoured company had largely been replaced as BCT's scrap merchant by a number of South Yorkshire-based bus dismantlers. On 7 August 1968, three engineless Birmingham buses stand in Long Marston with a number of British Railways carriages parked on their scrap line in the background. The two outer buses are Crossley-bodied Crossley DD42/6s 2307 (JOJ 307) and 2283 (JOJ 283), which had arrived for dismantling in January 1968 and May 1967 respectively, with the body of the latter already dismantled. Sandwiched between is 1667 (HOV 667), a Brush-bodied Leyland Titan PD2/1Sp, which had arrived at the same time as 2307. (D. R. Harvey)

2338 (JOJ 338)

Below: Three Crossley DD42/6s with Crossley H30/24R bodies are parked along the side of Quinton Garage next to Ridgacre Road in the spring of 1967. 2338 (JOJ 338), withdrawn on 28 February 1967, has recently arrived as it still has its front destination blind. It had spent its entire seventeen years in service operating from Acocks Green Garage and differed from the two other buses by having half-drop saloon windows. Both it and 2365 (JOJ 365) would be sold in January 1967 to Bird's for scrapping whereas 2366 would shortly be removed by Hudley of Wolverhampton and scrapped after June 1967. Both 2365 and 2366 had been withdrawn from Parry Barr Garage on 31 January 1967. (A. A. Turner)

2376 (JOJ 376)
Above: With 'NO WATER' signs neatly placed in their windscreens, five Crossley DD42/6s stand de-licensed in Lea Hall Garage yard, being among the last of these exposed radiator buses to be withdrawn on 30 September 1967. These fine buses, without a scratch on them, despite having synchromesh rather than preselector gearbox and the somewhat delicate 8.6-litre Crossley HOE7/4B engine, had been at Perry Barr Garage and all would be sold to Wombwell Diesels in March 1968. From right to left are 2376, 2394, 2374, 2382 and 2386, all with matching JOJ-registrations. (V. France)

2404 (JOJ 404)
Below: A number of these buses parked up and waiting to be collected from Washwood Heath Garage yard on 27 June 1965 have accident-damaged bodywork, including 2383 (JOJ 383), the Crossley on the extreme right. It always seemed a pity that the last twenty-three of the ultimate in exposed radiator Crossley DD42/6s were all taken out of service as their CoFs had expired and were deemed surplus to requirements. They had the much improved Crossley HOE7/5B 8.6-litre Crossley engine that was put into the entire last 100 'New Look' front Crossleys. 2404 (JOJ 404), on the right, also went to Smith. On the left is 1650 (GOE 650), which was one of ten pre-production Crossley DD42/6s and dated from 1 July 1949. Without its Crossley engine it has been taken out of service on 30 June 1964 and went to Smith of Stopsley near Luton. Also destined to be broken up by Smith is 2093 (JOJ 93), a MCCW-bodied Daimler CVD6, which was formerly allocated to Yardley Wood Garage for fourteen years until it was withdrawn on 31 March 1965. (R. Manison)

9
Post-War Buses, 1950–1960

2426 (JOJ 426)
What a change in fortunes! The trailblazing 2426 (JOJ 426) was the very first Crossley DD42/6 to have a concealed radiator. This long front cowling was known as the 'New Look' after Christian Dior's radical early post-war skirt length, with its hipped waist and long fitted length. When new on 24 February 1950, the bus body was finished to exhibition standards and even sported a step on the nearside front of the concealed radiator cover in order for shorter mechanics to check the water levels in the radiator. 2426 was initially operated on the 1A route, which passed General Manager Mr A. C. Baker's house in Wake Green Road so that he could see his 'star' bus. Despite its provenance, 2426 was among the first of the class to be withdrawn, this taking place on 31 July 1968. (G. Yates)

2437 (JOJ 437)
Above: Parked in the former tramway permanent way yard in Miller Street are the remains of 2437 (JOJ 437). This Crossley-bodied Crossley was working on the Inner Circle 8 route at the Whitehead Road and Alma Street junction on 11 October 1963 when it collided with another bus working on the 7 route and turned over. Forty-nine passengers were taken to hospital, but fortunately there were no fatalities. From early in 1964 the bus, devoid of its running units, was used as a turn-over practice vehicle before being sold for scrap to Bird's (although it was not collected until November 1966). Alongside the Crossley is 1531 (GOE 531), a Daimler CVA6 and 1945 (HOV 945), a 1949-built Daimler CVD6, both buses having Metro Cammell bodywork. (L. Mason)

2465 (JOJ 465)
Below: 2465 (JOJ 465), a 1950-built Crossley DD42/6 with a Crossley H30/24R body, was the first bus to replace the 65 tram route to Short Heath in the late morning of Saturday 4 July 1953. It had started off its operational life as one of only about ten 'New Look' front Crossleys to be allocated to Acocks Green Garage but in readiness for the Erdington tramway conversion scheme was moved to Miller Street Garage, where it remained with a brief sojourn at Selly Oak until withdrawn on 31 March 1969. By now devoid of its radiator cover, 2465 stands in Washwood Heath Garage yard prior to being sold to Wombwell Diesels in September 1969. (A. Yates)

2475 (JOJ 475)

Above: Stripped down to its frame and surrounded by former London Transport RT class buses, the almost unrecognisable remains of 2475 (JOJ 475) are standing in the yard of Wombwell Diesels in the late summer of 1970. These Crossley-bodied Crossley DD42/6s buses almost certainly would not have been withdrawn as BCT had earmarked most of these last 100 'New Look' front buses to be kept running until 1971. But the newly set up WMPTE wanted rid of manual gearboxes and the Crossleys and many of the surviving Park Royal-bodied Leyland Titan PD2s had to go. 2475 was withdrawn on 31 March 1969, but was stored by WMPTE until it was sold to Wombwell Diesels in June 1970. (R. F. deBöer)

2489 (JOJ 489)

Below: The only Birmingham Crossley not to be sold for scrap is 2489 (JOJ 489). The best one of six kept off the sales lists, 2489 was intended to be a driver-training bus, but with the scheme aborted by the incoming WMPTE management, it was considered to be the best of the six and was bought for the princely sum of £129, plus the tyres. The Crossley DD42/6 has a Crossley H30/24R body and was new in July 1950, being withdrawn on 31 March 1969. In early October 1969 it is parked at the open ground on the corner of Frankley Beeches Road and Bristol Road South, Northfield, literally days after it left Liverpool Street Garage for the last time, where it had been in store for six months. It is still going strong at the time of writing! (PM Photography)

2516 (JOJ 516)

Above: At the Festival of Britain, 2516 (JOJ 516), which had previously exhibited at the 1950 Commercial Motor Show at Earls Court, was put on display from 13 June until 18 July 1951 as an example of the best in British bus design and engineering. It had been in service in Birmingham for six months and, after several days of heated correspondence, 2516 was given a complete repaint at ACV's expense, as well as a free set of new tyres. It is parked at the head of a line of other withdrawn buses in early 1970 – a shadow of its former pristine self as it awaits collection by Wombwell Diesels. (R. F. deBöer)

2532 (JOJ 532)

Below: With its half-shafts already removed, 2532 (JOJ 532) stands in Lea Hall Garage yard on 5 February 1974, having been withdrawn on New Year's Eve 1973. The bus had entered service from Quinton Garage on 1 August 1950, but after being taken over on 1 October 1969 eventually finished its career at Washwood Heath Garage. The Metro-Cammell bodies were similar to those on the 2031 class of Daimler CVD6s. Unlike the earlier post-war bodies, they had a slightly extended upper saloon and a recessed windscreen that married up to the front profile and the by now standard triple indicator destination display layout. The buses gradually had the term 'Birmingham Standard' applied to all BCT concealed radiator classes. These 100 Guy Arab III Sp buses were very long-lived, with four lasting until the last day of ex-BCT rear-platform bus operation on 31 October 1977. (D. R. Harvey Collection)

2564 (JOJ 564)

Above: These six withdrawn former Birmingham City Transport buses are lined up in Adderley Street yard on 23 February 1975. These buses would all be late purchases of W. T. Bird, who bought them all for scrapping at their Long Marston site. On the left are 2564 (JOJ 564) and 2542 (JOJ 542), a pair of 26-foot-long MCCW-bodied Guy Arab III Sp dating from 1950. In the middle is 2787 (JOJ 787), a Daimler CVG6 with a Crossley body, and next it is 2967 (JOJ 967), a 1952-built 27-foot-long Guy Arab IV Sp, also bodied by Metro-Cammell, while on the right is 3029 (MOF 29), another Guy Arab IV Sp, which is the only one still with its radiator grill still attached. (D. R. Harvey Collection)

2585 (JOJ 585)

Below: 2585 (JOJ 585) was an early withdrawal from the 2526 class of Guy Arab III Sp, being taken out of service on 31 January 1966 after being involved in a severe accident that wrote off most of the platform and staircase. It has already been stripped of its bonnet and concealed radiator assembly and waits its removal from Lea Hall Garage yard by Hoyles of Wombwell in September 1966. On the left is 2383 (JOJ 383), a Crossley-bodied Crossley DD42/6 that had also been written-off after an accident, having been withdrawn on 30 April 1965. (D. R. Harvey Collection)

2608 (JOJ 608)
Above: 2608 (JOJ 608) stands in Holford Drive in February 1953, its Metro-Cammell body having suffered serious damage following a collision with a BRS lorry and trailer at the junction of Bradford Street and Rea Street while working the last Night Service 44 route to Acocks Green on 30 January 1953. As well as the contorted front and nearside, the rear body panels were distorted and the platform and staircase were both written-off. However, all is not what it seems, for 2608 was eventually repaired at Tyburn Road Works using many new body parts obtained from Metro-Cammell and was not withdrawn until 1972! (B. C. T.)

2615 (JOJ 615)
Below: Parked up ready for another day's service in the rear of Acocks Green garage are 26-foot-long Guy Arab III Sps 2615 (JOJ 615) and 2600 (JOJ 600), with 3100 (MOF 100), a 27-foot-long Guy Arab IV Sp, parked on the right. In fact, it is Sunday 1 November 1977 and these three buses completed their last ever day's service on the Outer Circle 11 route the previous day. That was the last day of the Birmingham Standards and all three buses would be auctioned for scrapping in February 1978. (D. R. Harvey)

2645 (JOJ 645)

2645 (JOJ 645) was one of a handful of the 1951-built Daimler CVD6s to be transferred to Park Lane Garage, Wolverhampton, immediately after the formation of WMPTE. These Daimlers were in good order but were becoming surplus to requirements in Birmingham due in no small part to their poor engine oil usage. 2645 was withdrawn in September 1970 and, after being left at Park Lane Garage yard, it was sold to Wombwell Diesels for scrap in November 1970 after being involved in an accident with a lorry that virtually destroyed the offside lower saloon. (D. R. Harvey Collection)

2681 (JOJ 681)

Standing in Miller Street Garage yard in August 1970 after their recent withdrawal are five Daimler CVD6s with MCCW H30/24R bodywork, all of which entered service on 1 August 1951. 2681 (JOJ 681) is fitted with one of BCTs ugly replacement fibreglass radiator grills. It had been withdrawn on 28 February 1970, as were 2656 (JOJ 681), 2677 (JOJ 681) and 2674 (JOJ 681). 2681 was sold to Hudley, Bilston for scrap in June 1971, while 2656 and 2677 went to Wombwell Diesels for scrap in November 1971 and 2674 went to Sykes, Blackerhill, for scrap in June 1971. (J. Blake)

2705 (JOJ 705)

2705 (JOJ 705), a Daimler CVD6 with MCCW H30/234R bodywork that entered service on 1 September 1951, has recently been withdrawn as it stands parked alongside a concealed radiator Crossley in late 1969. 2705 only survived with WMPTE for one month before being taken out of service and was quickly sold to Hartwood Finance in March 1970. This class of 150 buses were the first in the fleet to be 27 feet long – the extra length being used to enlarge the platform area. All previous Birmingham metal-framed body orders had the bodies built in two halves, but these buses were the first standard BCT design to have one-piece metal-framed bodywork. This tidied up the side of the buses, removing the between-decks guttering, while the depth of the windows in each saloon was increased. (D. R. Harvey Collection)

2728 (JOJ 728)

Above: Lea Hall Garage yard had become a useful storage space for withdrawn buses. In July 1971, 2728 (JOJ 728), 2681 (JOJ681), 2720 (JOJ 720) and 2674 (JOJ 674), the latter having been recently moved from Miller Street yard, wait for their respective purchasers to take them away for scrapping. Only 2674 shows any sign of vandalism, with most of its lower-saloon windows being broken. (D. R. Harvey Collection)

2821 (JOJ 821)

Below: After the Midland Red company's West Midlands area services were taken over by WMPTE on 3 December 1973, the extensive Adderley Street yard, opposite the entrance to Liverpool Street Garage, which was formerly used for overspill bus parking from Digbeth Garage, was used to dump withdrawn buses from about 1975. On 17 July 1977, the barely tarmacked surface was already quite full with buses awaiting collection by the scrap dealers who had bought them at auction. By this date most buses entering Adderley Street Yard never came out as a runner, unlike ten years previously, when many buses were driven under their own power to the scrapyard. 2821 (JOJ 821), a Crossley-bodied Daimler CVG6, entered service on 1 August 1952 and was withdrawn on 31 August 1976 after the withdrawal of former BCT Standards from both of the last two cross-city services from South Yardley to Hamstead and from Solihull to Collingwood Drive, Aldridge, that during 1976. Behind it is 2624 (JOJ 624), a 1951 Guy Arab III Sp that was withdrawn on 30 May 1977 from Acocks Green Garage. (D. R. Harvey Collection)

2790 (JOJ 790)

Above: Half shafts having been removed and a distorted nearside front wing all suggest that the end is nigh for 2790 (JOJ 790), a Daimler CVG6 with a Crossley H30/25R body. This bus was one of the first half of an order for 250 of this type and this bus entered service on 1 July 1952, in time for the Bristol Road and Cotteridge tram conversions. These JOJ-registered buses took exactly twelve months to be delivered and all the buses in the class were taken over by WMPTE in October 1969. 2790 was withdrawn on 31 May 1976 and was sold to Rollinson, Carlton, in July 1976. (A. J. Douglas)

2837 (JOJ 837)

Below: The derelict 2837 (JOJ 837) is parked inside Perry Barr Garage next to 2607 (JOJ 607), a Guy Arab III Sp, and 2819 (JOJ 819), a Daimler CVG6. This was a pair of buses converted to mobile Travelcard buses in October 1972 and given service fleet numbers 194 and 195 respectively. 2837, a Daimler CVG6 with a Crossley H30/25R body, was taken out of service on 31 December 1973 and sold to Hartwood, Blackerhill for scrap in May 1974. (A. Yates)

2876 (JOJ 876)

About to be hitched up to Paul Sykes's towing lorry in Adderley Street yard in the spring of 1972 is 2876 (JOJ 876). This was a Daimler CVG6 with a Crossley H30/25R body, which was new in February 1953 and which had been taken out of service after receiving severe accident damage to the rear platform area. The Gardner 6LW engine had already been removed prior to its disposal as there was still a demand for these second-hand engines. The towing vehicle had been converted from former London Transport RT 4761 (OLD 548). (A. Yates)

2883 (JOJ 883)

A rather battered 2883 (JOJ 883) awaits collection in Adderley Street yard by Rollinson, Carlton, after it was sold to them during February 1978. What was unusual about this Daimler CVG6 was that it was originally taken out of service on 31 August 1971. It was then placed in the WMPTE Ancillary Fleet three weeks later and given the fleet number 96. It was used as a driver-trainer for the next six years and was finally withdrawn on 31 October 1977 – a date which coincided with the final operation of Birmingham Standards on the Outer Circle 11 route. (Bristol VBG)

2903 (JOJ 903)

On Sunday 1 November 1977, the day after the final Birmingham Standards were withdrawn from the Outer Circle 11 route, most of the buses were parked at the rear of Acocks Green Garage. 2903 (JOJ 903), a Guy Arab IV Sp with a Gardner 6LW engine and a Metro-Cammell H30/25R body, was put into service from Selly Oak Garage on 1 July 1952, when it was used to replace tramcars on the Bristol Road services. After its withdrawal, 2903 was soon driven away for storage before being sold to scrap dealer D. Rollinson after February 1978. Next to it is former Coventry Corporation 220 (VWK 220), a Daimler CVG6 with a MCCW H33/27R body that was new in June 1958 and used on the Outer Circle route from August 1975 to augment elderly former BCT buses. (D. R. Harvey)

2924 (JOJ 924)
Above: 2924 (JOJ 924), a Guy Arab IV Sp with a Metro-Cammell body, was badly damaged on 26 March 1966. This Cotteridge Garage-based bus was involved in an accident with another vehicle and then ricocheted into Stitchley's Post Office in Pershore Road when working on the 45 route. The extreme damage to the cab and the offside of the body was considered so severe that it was officially withdrawn five days later and sold in June 1966 to Wombwell Diesels. (D. R. Harvey Collection)

2926 (JOJ 926)
Below: 2926 (JOJ 926), a Guy Arab IV Sp with a Metro-Cammell body, which was new on 1 July 1952, was rebuilt as part of an experiment to see if the standard BCT-style straight staircase could be replaced with a more compound layout. 2926 was fitted with a twin-turn staircase and its staircase window was removed. It was re-seated to H32/25R and fitted with Auster front and side ventilators, which considerably altered its appearance. The bus re-entered service on 18 July 1956, continuing its service operating from Cotteridge Garage. It was withdrawn early due to its non-standard layout at the end of January 1972. It is well on its way to be broken up when seen on 13 July 1972 at the Hudley Treading Company in Wednesbury. (E. V. Trigg)

2934 (JOJ 934)

Having been driven to Rollinson's yard in Barnsley, 2934 (JOJ 934) is still largely complete in the spring of 1978. This Metro-Cammell-bodied Guy Arab IV Sp was new in September 1952 and was taken out of service in September 1977, just one month before the final buses of this type were withdrawn in Birmingham. Behind 2934 is an unidentified BMMO D9 double-decker, one of many purchased from WMPTE by Rollinson of Carlton. (D. R. Harvey Collection)

2961 (JOJ 961)

Standing on the forecourt of Quinton Garage is 2961 (JOJ 961). Although structurally still intact, it is minus its front wheels and most of its running units have been taken off the bus, which had been in store for over six months. This Metro-Cammell-bodied Guy Arab IV Sp was taken out of service on 31 October 1977 following the conversion of the Outer Circle 11 route to rear-engined bus operation. Having been bought at auction in March 1978, it is being taken away by one of Booth's of Rotherham trucks on 4 May 1978. (D. R. Harvey Collection)

2969 (JOJ 969)

Awaiting a prospective buyer, 2969 (JOJ 969) is parked at Birmingham Car Auctions in Balsall Heath. On 7 December 1978 it was about to be sold for scrap to Rollinson of Carlton. The nearside of the Metro-Cammell-bodied Guy Arab IV Sp has a banner advertisement between the decks for *Jubilee Street*, a BBC television programme made as part of HM the Queen's Diamond Jubilee celebrations, for which purpose it was on loan to the Pebble Mill Studios in August 1977. Only the lower front and nearside has been repainted to act as a background for the programme. (T. W. W. Knowles)

3006 (MOF 6)

Above: Dumped at the rear of Lea Hall Garage on 14 November 1973 is 3006 (MOF 6), a Guy Arab IV Sp with a MCCW H30/25R, which entered service on 1 July 1953 and was withdrawn on 31 August 1973. The bodies on these 1953-built buses were built in one unit and are discernible by not having the inter deck guttering, as seen on 2535 (JOJ 535), just to the rear. Alongside it is an earlier Guy Arab III Sp with some evidence of front-end accident damage. This bus dated from 3 August 1950 and had been withdrawn from Washwood Heath Garage on 30 September 1973. Some evidence of vandalised windows is visible on 3006 – something that ten years earlier would have been virtually unheard of. Both buses were dispatched to Hartwood Finance for scrap in May 1974. (D. R. Harvey Collection)

3017 (MOF 17)

Below: The remains of 3017 (MOF 17) stand in the yard of Passenger Vehicle Sales, near Barnsley, in the spring of 1977. It is well on the way to being broken up, although the Gardner 6LW engine is still in place. 3017, a Metro-Cammell-bodied Guy Arab IV Sp, had been new to Miller Street on 1 July 1953 as a tram replacement bus for the final Erdington group of tram services just four days later. It was withdrawn on 31 May 1975 and then spent nearly two years in store. This was one of the second half of the order for 27-foot-long Guy Arab IVs with the usual floor-mounted Wilson pre-selector gearbox, and were identical to the 2901 class. All the class passed into WMPTE ownership on 1 October 1969. (D. R. Harvey Collection)

3067 (MOF 67)
Above: Parked after withdrawal in Quinton Garage yard in early 1972 is the still intact 3067 (MOF 67). This was one of five of this class of Guy Arab IV Sps bodied by Metro-Cammell that entered service on 1 January 1954, nominally replacing pre-war Daimler COG5s. 3067 was sold to Wombwell Diesels for scrap in September 1972, not necessarily because there was something amiss with it, but rather that it was not considered to be worthwhile issuing it with another short-term CoF when WMPTE were purchasing new Daimler Fleetlines. This policy would rebound on the PTE as industrial action would affect the whole of the bus industry and the delivery of new vehicles would be reduced to a trickle. (D. R. Harvey)

3100 (MOF 100)
Below: On 31 October 1977 the last Birmingham Standards were withdrawn when the final crew-operated route in Birmingham, the famous 26-mile-long Outer Circle, was converted to One-Man-Operation (OMO). Some of the Birmingham buses were twenty-seven years old and this bus, 3100 (MOF 100), which entered service on 1 October 1954, was a mere youngster at twenty-three years old. This Guy Arab IV Sp with a MCCW H30/25R body is parked at the rear of Acocks Green Garage the day after it had come out of service. (D. R. Harvey)

3117 (MOF 117)

3117 (MOF 117) was one of the second half of the order for 125 Crossley-bodied Daimler CVG6s, though many of them were stored for three months or more until most of the last of the pre-war buses were withdrawn. These 27-foot-long buses were the same as the 2776 class. 3117 has been abandoned in Lea Hall Garage yard on 17 October 1971 without its engine and gearbox. The nearside front corner of the Crossley body has been pushed in and deemed not worthy of reconstruction. (J. Carroll)

3146 (MOF 146)

A pair of Daimler CVG6s, 3146 (MOF 146) and 3153 (MOF 153), are parked in Perry Barr Garage yard in 1973. 3146 was withdrawn on 30 November 1972 while 3153 went on 30 April 1973, and both were sold in August 1973 to Paul Sykes, Blackerhill. It was always noticeable that earlier arrivals at any parking site were stripped first, although sometimes one wondered why the buses supposedly becoming the recipient of the spares actually need them, as often they too were shortly to be doomed to meet with the scrap man's oxyacetylene torch. (D. A. Yates)

3181 (MOF 181)

Above: Once WMPTE had taken over the BCT fleet, and even though many survived well into the mid-1970s, the rule of thumb was to take major accident victims out of service, whereas only a few years earlier they probably would have been repaired. Crossley-bodied Daimler CVG6 3181 (MOF 181) was withdrawn on 3 July 1972 after being involved in an accident when working on a Night Service 5 service. The damage to 3181 wrote off the concealed radiator, but this was merely superficial; the offside front wheel standing on a thick plank of wood at a slightly odd angle is the real reason for the vehicle's withdrawal. (D. A. Yates)

3188 (MOF 188)

Below: 3188 (MOF 188) stands in Perry Barr yard after it had been withdrawn on 31 August 1973. Although looking like any other standard Crossley-bodied Daimler CVG6, it had acted as a prototype for the future deliveries of Daimler Fleetline CRG6LXs. 3188 gained fluorescent saloon lighting inside long, tubular modules and yellow-painted ceilings in November 1960. It has already lost its radiator grill and an attempt to remove the offside rear wing. Nearly two years later it was purchased for scrap by Bird's of Long Marston. (D. R. Harvey Collection)

3196 (MOF 196)
Hartwood Finance purchased all three of these Daimler CVG6s in May 1974 and each have the chalked markings 'A1' in the lower-saloon front window signifying who purchased them. 3196 (MOF 196), dating from 1 July 1954, had been withdrawn on 31 July 1973, while next to it is 3219 (MOF 219), which was taken out of service at the end of October 1973. On the right, 2844 (JOJ 844), which entered service on 1 November 1952, was a more recent withdrawal, being withdrawn on 31 January 1974. (D. R. Harvey Collection)

3227 (MOF 227)
Numerically the very last BCT Standard to be ordered was Crossley-bodied Daimler CVG6 3227 (MOF 227), which is parked in Perry Barr on 15 July 1977. The last eleven of these buses were stored in the former Witton tram depot for three months until most of the last of the pre-war buses were withdrawn. 3227 was always regarded as an unlucky bus, being involved in a number of fatal accidents. Despite this it was earmarked for preservation, but after another front-end accident towards the end of June 1977 it was sold to PVS Spares, Barnsley, in September 1977. (D. R. Harvey Collection)

3228 (9 JML)
Above: There were five prototype 30-foot-long low-height integral Bridgemasters and the second Crossley Bridgemaster MB2RA to be built had a Crossley H41/31R body that was one of only two fitted with flat window pans. 3228 (9 JML) was exhibited in the Demonstrator Park at the 1956 Earl's Court Commercial Motor Show. It originally had the small AEC AV 470 7.685-litre engine coupled to a synchromesh gearbox, but on 9 March 1965 the larger AEC AV.590 9.6-litre engine was fitted. It was demonstrated to BCT between 13 February and 1 August 1957, when it was purchased by BCT from ACV Sales Ltd, Southall. Given the fleet number 3228, 9 JML was purchased in order to trial a 30-foot-long and 8-foot-wide double-decker, but was only allowed to operate after the platform staff and unions agreed to collect fares only if there were no standing passengers. This trailblazing agreement presaged the 'no standing rule' on all of BCT's subsequent 30-foot buses, although they were all rear-engined. It operated throughout its life from Lea Hall Garage until it was withdrawn in June 1969 and sold via Wombwell Diesels three months later to Edmunds Omnibus Services Ltd, Rassau, who ran it until May 1971 in an ever increasingly depressing appearance. It is with Edmunds in early 1971 prior to being withdrawn. (D. R. Harvey Collection)

2211 MK
Below: The second attempt by ACV to get an order for their chassis-less AEC Bridgemaster was with the first forward-entrance to be built. 2211 MK was the 2B3RA model, which had the larger AEC AV 590 9.6-litre engine. It still had a synchromesh gearbox, which in a largely pre-selector fleet won few friends among the drivers at Lea Hall Garage, where it was demonstrated to BCT between 14 June 1960 and 2 May 1961. The bus was fitted with a rather stark-looking metal-framed Park Royal H43/29F body. It was seen carrying the fleet number 3229, suggesting that it was already BCT property, but it was returned to ACV who then sold it to G. W. Osborne, Tollesbury, Essex, later that year. It survived in Essex being a regular on the service to Colchester until it was withdrawn. It is parked at Essex County Cricket Club's Chelmsford Ground in the late 1980s, where it was used as their souvenir shop. (S. Calder)

10

Rear-Engined Buses

3230 (460 MTE)
The Leyland Atlantean PDR1/1, 460 MTE, was new as a Leyland demonstrator, having been on loan to Birmingham when it was fitted with a Leyland 0.600 engine during February 1960. It returned to Birmingham on extended loan from 21 September 1960, this time having been fitted with an O.680 'Power Plus' 11.1-litre engine. It was acquired on 1 May 1961 and numbered 3230. It was converted to OMO on 2 May 1973 with a revised front destination box that was lowered so that the driver could change the destination display. Originally allocated to Rosebery Street and Hockley Garage, it spent most of its life at Yardley Wood Garage, where it is parked after withdrawal in March 1978 without its engine. 3230 was sold to D. Rollinson, Carlton, for scrap on 29 March 1979. (R. A. Mills)

3233 (233 DOC)

Above: Stripped of its engine and body parts, 3233 (233 DOC) is dumped in Adderley Street yard on 11 October 1977. Even the offside upper-saloon front windows have been removed, possibly for future use. 3233 had entered service along with the rest of the class numbered 3231–3240 on Bonfire Night 1961 and was a MCCW H39/33F-bodied Leyland Atlantean PDR1/1. It had a pneumocyclic gearbox, an entrance in front of the front axle and a generously low seating capacity, although in 1969 all were converted to H43/33F. These were the last Birmingham buses to have tungsten light bulbs and originally retained the standard BCT front destination box layout. It was converted to OMO on 14 February 1973, as evident by the low-mounted destination boxes. It survived until 30 June 1977 and was sold to Hartwood Finance, Birdwell, by February 1978. (D. R. Harvey Collection)

3245 (245 DOC)

Below: The first ten prototype Daimler Fleetline CRG6LXs were mainly delivered in February 1962 and had MCCW H39/33F bodies. 3245 (245 DOC) passed to WMPTE on 1 October 1969 and was withdrawn on 31 December 1977. It was converted into a driver recruitment vehicle and mobile cinema in February 1979 before becoming a towing vehicle in 1983. Withdrawn on 4 April 1986, it was used as a turnover vehicle until at least June 1987, whereupon its remains were scrapped by WMPTE. With its front windows boarded up as part of its conversion into a recruitment bus, and formerly painted with a large, cheery driver's face, it is dumped in Perry Barr Garage yard on 11 April 1987. (D. R. Harvey)

3249 (249 DOC)

Above: Chassis numbers 60004–60013 were some of the first Daimler Fleetline CRG6LXs supplied to any operator. The earliest was the demonstrator, with chassis number 60000, which was supplied to BCT as 7000 HP and that operated from new in December 1960 and into the following January from Lea Hall Garage. 3249 (249 DOC) entered service on 20 January 1962 and unlike the earlier ten trial Leyland Atlanteans was never converted to OMO as slightly lowered driver operated destination gear could not be fitted. As a result, the buses retained their triple indicator blind layout until withdrawal. 3249 was withdrawn on 30 September 1977 and was sold to Rollinson's of Carlton. It stands at the entrance to Perry Barr Garage in early 1978 with its Gardner 6LX engine already removed, but unusually its rear chassis member has not yet been cut off. (D. R. Harvey Collection)

3262 (262 GON)

Below: Awaiting its fate in 1978 in Adderley Street yard is Park Royal-bodied Daimler Fleetline CRG6LXs 3262 (262 GON), dating from August 1963. It had been taken out of service on 31 August 1977 after being damaged in an accident and considered to be beyond economic repair. The body contract for BCT's initial order for 300 Daimler Fleetline CRG6LX chassis was split between Metro-Cammell and, somewhat surprisingly, Park Royal. The bodies had a new style destination box layout, which, although retaining separate destination and number boxes, had them mounted alongside each other. It was sold to Rollinson of Carlton in December 1978 for scrap. Alongside it is 3405 (405 KOV), identical to 3262 but almost exactly a year younger, which had another years' service in front of it. (Bristol VBG)

3278 (278 GON)

3278 (278 GON) was a Daimler Fleetline CRG6LX with a Park Royal H39/33F body and had entered service from Coventry Road Garage on 16 September 1963. The Park Royal bodies could be distinguished from the MCCW ones by their curved rear dome and the flat-bottomed panel beneath the driver's cabside windows. All were re-seated to H43/33F during 1967. It had been withdrawn on New Year's Eve 1978 and is waiting to be collected from Adderley Street yard by Rollinson's towing lorry. (D. R. Harvey Collection)

3281 (281 GON)

Carrying on from where Daimler COG5 617 (AOG 617) and Crossley DD42/6 2437 (JOJ 437) had left off, 3281 (281 GON) was briefly used as a practice turnover bus at the rear of Lea Hall Garage in the summer of 1979. Stripped of all body parts, the shell is literally at its 'tipping point' during one such recovery practice. 3281 was a Daimler Fleetline CRG6LX with a Park Royal H43/33F body that had entered service on 16 September 1963. It was sold to T. Wigley of Carlton in August 1979, some five months after being taken out of service. (R. A. Mills)

3339 (339 GON)

It was the policy of WMPTE to not only sell buses for scrap without their engines, but also to cut-off the rear section of the chassis. This meant that the bus could not be used again by an operator and ensured that the bus would be broken up. 3339 (339 GON), a Daimler Fleetline CRG6LX with a MCCW body, parked in Adderley Street yard, had received this treatment after its withdrawal from service on 1 March 1979, so that its purchaser, Booth's of Rotherham, was compelled to scrap the bus. (D. R. Harvey Collection)

Rear-Engined Buses

3336 (336 GON)
Above: Recently parked up in Washwood Heath Garage yard is 3336 (336 GON). With blinds removed and some lower-saloon windows smashed, it has had its fleet number and ownership details painted out, although attempts to hide its identity have been somewhat spoilt by the number plate still being affixed. This MCCW-bodied Daimler Fleetline CRG6LX dated from 1 October 1963 and spent its entire life operating from Washwood Heath Garage, mainly on the 55 and 56 services. It was withdrawn on 31 March 1979 and went to Wigley's of Carlton just over five months later. (D. R. Harvey Collection)

3354 (354 KOV)
Below: Along with two dumped, unidentified former Kingston-upon-Hull Corporation Leyland 'Atlantean' PDR1/1s, 3354 (354 KOV), a Daimler Fleetline CRG6LX with a MCCW H39/33F body, new to Moseley Road Garage on 6 June 1964, is in Adderley Street yard in 1979. It had been withdrawn at the end of April 1979 and was quickly stripped of its Gardner 6LX engine before being despatched to Whitings of Pontefract in August 1979. On the left is former Midland Red 5286 (5286 HA), a 1963 Daimler Fleetline CRG6LX with an Alexander H44/33F body, which was taken over by West Midlands PTE on 3 December 1973. (D. R. Harvey Collection)

3374 (374 KOV)
Above: With most of its offside front wrecked due to a severe accident, 3374 (374 KOV), a 1964 Daimler Fleetline CRG6LX with a MCCW body, is ready for Rollinson's towing lorry for the one-way trip to South Yorkshire. It had been taken out of service on 28 February 1978 as a result of this smash and was slowly stripped of any useful spares before going for scrap that December. It is standing in Adderley Street yard having been deemed uneconomic to repair, as buses of this vintage were already being earmarked for early withdrawal. (D. R. Harvey Collection)

3440 (440 KOV)
Below: Recently withdrawn on 31 March 1980, 3440 (440 KOV) stands in the yard of Quinton Garage in 1981. Unlike other garages, Quinton only ever stored withdrawn buses rather than stripping them for spares, and thus buses standing alongside the garage were only 'in transit'. Having entered service on 14 September 1964 from Perry Barr Garage, 3440, a MCCW-bodied Daimler Fleetline CRG6LX, is being stored before being sent to Moseley Road Garage in February 1982 for use in the Apprentices' Training School for disassembly by the trainees. (A. Whitehouse)

3453 (BON 453C)

Above: 3453 (BON 453C) is standing next to Quinton Garage after its withdrawal on 31 April 1979 along with 3452 (BON 452C). These buses were the first-ever Daimler Fleetline CRG6LXs to be bodied as single-deckers were the twenty-four that were fitted with Marshall B37F bodies. The ramp-floored Marshall body had an attractive BET Federation-style windscreen, but had a seating capacity of only thirty-seven. It was perhaps a shame that the 'bustle' was not incorporated into the body. This unusual purchase by BCT in 1965 was nominally to replace the Leyland Tiger PS2/1s of 1950 but in fact augmented them for about four more years. These were the first Fleetlines to be bodied as single-deckers and were the only ones to be designated CRG rather than the later SRG classification. The chassis had the standard 16-foot 3-inch wheelbase, though the bodies were slightly longer than normal at 30 foot 6 inches. 3453 would eventually be despatched to Booth, a Rotherham-based scrap dealer, in June 1980. (D. R. Harvey)

3479 (BON 479C)

Below: The engine shrouds have been taken off the chassis of 3479 (BON 479C), seen here parked in Perry Barr Garage soon after its withdrawal on 31 March 1980. Its survival after being taken out of service was a short one, as it was sold just three months later to Booth's of Rotherham for scrap. This Daimler Fleetline CRG6LX had a Park Royal body that was distinguishable from the contemporary Metro-Cammell body by having a more rounded rear dome. The rear view of the bus reveals the transverse Gardner 6LX 10.45-litre engine still in situ. The bus is facing the distant Alexander Greyhound Stadium in Aldridge Road. (D. R. Harvey Collection)

3550 (BON 550C)

Above: The Metro-Cammell-bodied Daimler Fleetline CRG6LXs, with the odd exception, were withdrawn almost en mass in 1980. 3550 (BON 550C) is parked in Adderley Street yard soon after being taken out of service. Once in the yard (which was just off High Street, Bordesley, and opposite Liverpool Street Garage) buses rarely, if ever, came out to operate again. 3550 entered service on New Year's Day 1966 and was withdrawn on 31 October 1980. Both it and fellow class member 3556 (BON 556C) – seen here with the destination blind 'LODE LANE' still in place – were sold to Askin of Barnsley for breaking up in September 1981. (R. Deloyde)

3625 (FOC 625D)

Below: Long since out of use judging by its grimy condition, 3625 (FOC 625D) is in Lea Hall Garage in February 1981. This Daimler Fleetline CRG6LX had a Park Royal H43/33F body and entered service in January 1967. It was the last bus delivered to BCT with a D suffix registration. These Park Royal bodies were the first built for BCT with the 1930s Dodson-style upper-saloon front windows, which considerably modernised these bodies. Noticeable with the doors open is the single step entrance, which enabled easy access for passengers. It was sold to Askin's of Barnsley in October 1981 and was broken up. (F. W. York)

3631 (JOB 631E)

Above: Parked after withdrawal, 3631 (JOB 631E) sits alongside 3645 (JOB 645E). These two Park Royal-bodied Daimler Fleetline CRG6LXs have already been sold as they have a buyer's sticker in the nearside windscreen. Dating from 1 February and 1 March 1967 respectively, both buses were taken out of service on 31 March 1981 and were sold in June 1981, with 3631 going to Booth's of Rotherham and 3645 to Wigley of Carlton. Alongside it is 3887 (SOE 887H), one of the 100 Daimler Fleetline CRG6LXs with 33-foot-long Park Royal eighty-seat dual-door bodywork. This bus entered service in October 1969, a few days after BCT were taken over by WMPTE. This bus entered service in the BCT dark blue and cream colours but without municipal crests. These buses were withdrawn early due to structural body problems; 3887 was one of the last six to be withdrawn and was also sold to Booth's in June 1981. (D. R. Harvey Collection)

3666 (KOX 666F)

Below: At the front of a line of withdrawn AEC Swift MP2Rs with an AEC AH505 8.2-litre engine is 3666 (KOX 666F). There were twelve of these shorter 33-foot-long single-deckers with MCW B37D bodies which could carry thirty-nine standee passengers. Initially, these buses were allocated to Acocks Green Garage for use on the inter-suburban 36 service that served the industrial areas of Tyseley and Small Heath, which was very busy in the morning and afternoon peak periods. These standee buses were not popular and were early candidates for withdrawal as a pilot mid-life overhaul was going to be far too expensive. As a result, they were withdrawn early, and three of them are lined up in Perry Barr Garage parking area in front of the garage, some three months after withdrawal in April 1977. All the Swifts were withdrawn during 1977, with 3666 being sold to Passenger Vehicle Spares of Carlton for scrap in November 1977. (D. R. Harvey)

3671 (KOX 671F)

Immediately after a complete bus was withdrawn, it was often the case that a random part was removed for no apparent reason! Here a single panel has been removed from the offside of the MCW body of this AEC Swift MP2R, which otherwise looks as though it was ready to go back into service. 3671 (KOX 671F) stands in Perry Barr Garage yard on 15 July 1977, around ten weeks after it had been taken out of service. (D. R. Harvey)

3675 (KOX 675F)

3675 (KOX 675F) was the first of the six 36-foot-long AEC Swift 2P2Rs that entered service on 1 October 1967 and was withdrawn on 31 July 1977. Their MCW bodies had an extra bay in front of the central exit door and could carry thirty-nine standing passengers. They also differed from the dozen shorter buses by having an AEC AH691 11.3-litre engine. 3675 is parked after withdrawal on 31 July 1977 in Selly Oak Garage. It was sold to Passenger Vehicle Spares of Carlton for scrap in February 1978. (F. W. York)

3751 (KOX 751F)

The burnt-out remains of 3751 (KOX 751F) sits alongside Lea Hall Garage on 14 November 1973, where it would eventually be dismantled. This 1968-built Park Royal-bodied Daimler Fleetline CRG6LX was the first of the class to be withdrawn and was all but destroyed by an electrical fire. There would be few useful spare parts left to salvage. (D. R. Harvey Collection)

3730 (KOX 730F)

Above: 3730 (KOX 730F) is parked alongside Moseley Road Garage in the early autumn of 1982, showing some evidence of remedial body repairs undertaken by the WMPTE Apprentice School. The bus is a Daimler Fleetline CRG6LX with a MCW H43/33F body and was the last of the class of fifty that were among the first to have a two-step entrance. It entered service on 4 December 1967 from Cotteridge Garage. Sold to the 3730 Preservation Group in October 1982, this bus went to another preservation society but it failed to survive and was sold for scrap to Rollinson of Carlton by May 1986. (D. R. Harvey Collection)

3748 (KOX 748F)

Below: Still basically intact, 3748 (KOX 748F), a 1968-vintage Park Royal-bodied Daimler Fleetline CRG6LX, is waiting for disposal on 3 April 1982. These buses were the last single-door buses delivered to Birmingham and were again built with a two-step entrance. The bus has been stripped of its electrical components but the engine pack appears to be intact. It is in the company of other members of the 3731–3780 class, delivered between January and April 1968, that are awaiting their fate. It had been withdrawn on 28 February 1982 and was sold to J. Sykes of Carlton seven months later. (F. W. York)

3802 (NOV 802G)

Above: After its withdrawal on 31 January 1983, 3802 (NOV 802G) was sold to Black Country Tours of Netherton in June of the same year. It was given the name 'Aynuk' (and yes there was an 'Ayli') and was fitted with a bar and perimeter seating for use as a beer bus for visiting Real Ale public houses in the Black Country. It was employed as such for sixteen years and was a common sight around the Dudley area, especially at weekends. It is seen here at a bus rally in its fully lined-out red and cream livery. It was later sold to preservationist Robert Smith to provide spare parts for 3880. (D. R. Harvey)

3811 (NOV 811G)

Below: 3811 (NOV 811G), a Daimler Fleetline CRG6LX with a dual-door Park Royal body, originally new to Cotteridge Garage on 8 December 1968, was withdrawn on 30 April 1983. It was sold the next month to the West Midlands Fire Service for use as a practice recovery vehicle at the Sutton Coldfield Fire Station and stands as a totally deformed wreck in May 1985. By the following year, not surprisingly, the body was beyond use and it was sold for scrap. (D. R. Harvey)

3842 (NOV 842G)

Above: 3842 (NOV 842G) was one of the 100 NOV-registered Daimler Fleetline CRG6LXs fitted with dual-door Park Royal H43/29D bodywork that were delivered between November 1968 and May 1969. Only 3819 and 3842 were sold for further PSV use, with 3842 being sold to de Courcey Travel in September 1985 after being briefly used by a Solihull independent. De Courcey operated the bus for just eleven months, despite it being fully repainted into their livery. (D. R. Harvey Collection)

3884 (SOE 884H)

Below: Standing engineless in Adderley Street yard, 33-foot-long Daimler Fleetline CRG6LX 3884 (SOE 884H) was withdrawn in March 1980 before being despatched to Askin's dealership in Barnsley three months later. 3884 was one of the first six of the 100 buses ordered by BCT that were delivered before WMPTE took over the Corporation's bus operations. 3884 was delivered on 16 September 1969 to Yardley Wood Garage and was licensed for training purposes. The buses had the new square-style bodywork built by Park Royal to the new Government Bus Grant specifications. With a seating capacity of eighty, this led to them becoming known as 'Jumbos'. (D. R. Harvey Collection)

ENDNOTE

Well, that wasn't too depressing a read after all, was it!

BIBLIOGRAPHY

The main source of statistical information comes from the PSV Circle fleet history PD24 (2015), *Birmingham City Transport*, and my own *Birmingham Buses at Work Parts I & II*, published by Silver Link in 2004 and 2006 respectively.
Also by the Author for Amberley Books:
Across Birmingham on the 29A
Belfast Trolleybuses
Birmingham Before the Electric Tram
Birmingham City Transport
Coventry Buses 1914–1946
Coventry Buses 1948–1974
Leicester Buses
Midland Red Double-Deckers
Midland Red Single-Deckers
The Other Midland Reds
Trams in West Bromwich
Walsall Trolleybuses 1931–1970
West Bromwich Corporation Buses

For similar titles please visit:
www.amberley-books.com
The fastest-growing local history, general history, transport and specialist interest history publisher in the UK.